The taste guides

Pier Francesco Listri

Art, cuisine and nature in

VENETO

Itineraries of foods, views, and festas

BONECHI
edizioni il Turismo
FIRENZE - 1954

© Copyright 2000 by Bonechi Edizioni
'Il Turismo' S.r.l.
Via dei Rustici, 5 - 50122 Firenze, Italy
Tel. (+39) 055 239.82.24/25
Fax (+39) 055 216366
E-mail: barbara@bonechi.com
         bbonechi@data.it
http://www.bonechi.com

Photos: Archivio della Bonechi Edizioni 'Il Turismo' S.r.l.; Archivio Millevolte Firenze; Roberto Ghedina; Archivio fotografico dell'A.P.T. n° 12 – Riviera degli Olivi (Lake Garda); Archivio fotografico A.P.T. n° 14 – Rovigo; Archivio fotografico A.P.T. n° 1 Dolomites; Archivio fotografico A.P.T. n° 2 Belluno, Feltre e Alpago; Archivio fotografico A.P.T. n° 9 Terme Euganee; Archivio fotografico A.P.T. n° 10 Vicenza (photo Dalla Pozza; C. Gerolimetto; Colorfoto; G. Bittante; Cevese); Archivio fotografico A.P.T. n° 11 Treviso.

Translated by: Glen Haybittle

Coordinator: Barbara Bonechi
Artwork: Antonio Tassinari
Editorial staff: Lorena Lazzari
Drawings: Barbara Barucci

Photolithography: Cartografica Ciulli, Florence
Paste-up: Fotolito Immagine, Florence
Printed by: Lito Terrazzi, Florence

ISBN 88-7204-401-4

The location of the works indicated herein refers to the date of publication.

VENETO

Belluno

Padova

Vicenza

Venezia

Verona

Rovigo

Treviso

Veneto, a region rich in treasures

Veneto is one of the most attractive and stimulating regions of Italy, both because it possesses in Venice one of the world's most culturally and historically rich cities and because it is blessed with a vast array of natural wonders. The entire region, in fact, is endowed with a munificent political and artistic tradition as well as possessing a wide range of natural resources — alpine mountain ranges, fertile hills and plains, long stretches of sandy beaches and, of course, the sea — which have always ensured a flourishing proliferation of human activity in the area. For those with a deep interest in culture, Veneto possesses points of interest which are largely unique to the area. It is, in fact, a region where both national and international customs and styles — from Roman to Gothic, from Renaissance to Baroque — all find expression in a multi-faceted tapestry which also bears traces of an Oriental influence as a result of Venice's trading relations with the Byzantine empire.

The reader of this guide will hopefully glean an idea of the charm and rich cultural heritage enjoyed by this region of Italy which if, in Venice, possesses a pivotal point in the artistic development of he western world, also boasts cities such as Padua, Verona, Vicenza, Treviso and Belluno that offer a great deal in terms of historical monuments and

VENETO: where nature excels itself

Veneto, notwithstanding the multi-faceted beauty of its various territories, faces and for a thousand years has faced the sea.
Today, its hundreds of kilometers of sandy beaches and pine forests along the Adriatic coast represent a golden asset for the region's tourist industry.

However, Veneto also possesses an alpine spirit thanks to its mountain ranges and, in particular, the Dolomites. Sobriety, strength of character, breathtaking landscapes, simple and rustic food – from polenta to grappa and the local cheeses – are among the features which give this region of Veneto its distintive character.

The Veneto region is also indebted for the diversity of its landscapes to the almost primitive natural wonderlands of the Polesine and Delta del Po.
Here, rare flora and fauna abound amidst a natural setting of rare beauty.

The golden blaze of the domes of San Marco reflects something of the glory of the old Venetian Republic which for centuries ruled the seas towards the East. Slowly, it also began to assimilate the other cities and castled towns of the area and today the heritage of the Serenissima's dominion has left its mark throughout the region.

and many centuries of historical splendor

The people of Veneto took the trees from the mountains to build ships in order to satisfy their adventurous spirit and venture out into the great unknown. And it was Venice's dominion of the waves which brought so much glory and wealth to the city over the centuries, in particular through the trade routes it established with the East and the wars it fought with the Turks. For centuries, the doge on his Bucintoro personified the regal grandeur of the Republic.

From the fifthteenth to the eighteenth century, Venice and Veneto enriched the artistic heritage of the western world thanks to its figurative art and in particular the great emphasis on color displayed therein. But there was also the architecture of Palladio, the sculpture of Canova, the theater of Ruzante and Goldoni and the music of Vivaldi to pay testament to the great artistic fervor and talent of the natives of this region.

One of the glories of Veneto is represented by the three thousand villas scattered throughout the region. Built by the important familes of the cities with an eye to recreating in a pastoral setting the luxuries they enjoyed in the city, these villas reached their artistic peak in the masterpieces designed by the great Veneto architect Palladio who so successfully created a harmony between the natural environment and his art.

Of all the centuries of Veneto civilization, the one which perhaps stands out in terms of festivals, costumes, color and exuberance is the eighteenth. This was a world of dandies, cads, courtesans and great dames all caught up in a general air of playful transgression which, in many ways, has spawned the masks and costumes of the world-famous modern-day Carnival.

works of art.
But Veneto is a region which also boasts a vast array of artistic masterpieces outside of the cities thanks largely to the many splendid examples of architectural design constituted by the villas scattered throughout the countryside. Fruit of the Renaissance and then, especially, the building boom of the seventeenth and eighteenth centuries, these villas represent the desire of the Venetian patricians to recreate in the countryside that aesthetic ideal of living conditions which they so brilliantly acheived in the city. There were also, of course, pratical considerations and all these villas, from the supreme masterpieces of Palladio to the more modest country homes of later years, were closely linked to agricultural considerations. There are, in fact, in the region more than three thousand of these villas, most of them restored, and a series of walks have been designed in order to visit a large number of them – an essential experience for anyone wanting to understand the true nature and spirit of the Veneto.
Veneto can also offer its visitors an exquisite and varied cuisine, ranging from the most simple of dishes such as polenta to the vast array of more elaborate fish and seafood-based recipes. These then are a few of the reasons why a stay in Veneto will provide even the most hardened traveller with a wealth of vibrant impressions and much food for thought.

The cuisine of the mountainous regions of Veneto enjoys an excellent reputation and is renowned for its creative simplicity. Polenta is perhaps the most famous of its specialities and the region also produces some tasty cheeses.

A MAP OF

Where mixed herbs play an integral part in the creation of recipes and the East still leaves its mark, Veneto offers an excellent and varied cuisine:

Endowed with vast fertile plains, Veneto is thus in a position to offer a great variety of fresh vegetables from which its cuisine obviously benefits. The area is especially renowned for its white asparagus and red-leaved chicory which are cultivated, above all, in the Treviso area.

Veneto cuisine, though varied, is also heavily influenced by the severe simplicity of its mountainous regions and hence chestnuts and flour play an important role in the eating habits of the local population. Grappa too holds a prestigious place in the produce of the area. This rather strong liquer is very charateristic of the Veneto and is now appreciated the world over.

VENETO CUISINE

fresh vegetables from its plains, fish from its lakes and the sea, grappa and polenta from its mountains. Delicious meals always characterized by semplicity and fresh produce.

Veneto wines are famous in Italy. The white wines of the region enjoy an especially high reputation, though even some of the reds and the spumanti (sparkling white wine) produced around Verona, Lake Garda and the hilly areas of the region are of excellent quality.

Lake trout, eels from the lagoons and various fish and seafood from the Adriatic all contribute to the local specialities of Veneto which however is headed by the baccalà (cod) and, in particular, the famous baccalà alla vicentina.

Veneto, maestro of alcoholic beverages

Wherever you happen to find yourself in the Veneto region, you can rest assured that there will be an excellent local wine on offer. The Veneto, in fact, is renowned for its high quality wines, some of which are exported all over the world. And the region produces a wide variety, from light white wines to strong full-bodied red wines and the potent grappa which is distilled from marc and has become famous throughout the world. The rich soil around Verona is responsible for famous wines like the white *Soave* and the delicate red *Bardolino*, the celebrated *Valpolicella* and, ideal with red mear, the prestigious *Amarone* and *Reciota*. The region of Vicenza is known for wines such as *Tarbalino*, *Torcolato di Breganze*, *Garganega* and *Gambellara*. In the Conegliano region recommended wines include the white *Prosecco* and *Cortizze* while in other areas the red *Cabernet*, the white *Pinot*, *Merlot* and *Tocai* are all first-rate wines. Many of these wines carry the prestigious DOC certification on their labels.
You'll find in this guide an area-by-area review of the local wines which are worth sampling.

Spotlight on FESTIVALS IN VENETO

In order to understand the history and character of Veneto better and sample its charms season by season.

The special events, month by month

CORTINA-DOBBIACO (the beginning of February): international grand slalom skiing tournament.

VENICE CARNIVAL (February): masks, costumes, parades in St Mark's square and on the gondolas. Ten days of wild fun and worldly elegance.

VENICE, FESTIVAL OF SAINT MARKS (April 25): Large festival in honour of Venice's patron saint with gondola races, "risi e bisi" (rice with peas) and free roses for lovers.

VENICE, REGATA DELLA SENSA (the second Sunday in May): Large ceremony for the traditional wedding of Venice with the sea, with the carrying out to sea of the laurel wreath followed by the splendid regatta on the Grand Canal.

VENICE, BIENNALE D'ARTE (every two years, from June to September): exhibition of modern art from around the world.

PADUA, SAGRA DI SANT'ANTONIO (June 13): Celebration in honour of Padua's patron saint which goes back centuries, with a large fair in Prato della Valle.

CORTINA, COPPA D'ORO DELLE DOLOMITI (second half of July): International veteran sports car race attracting competitors from all over the world.

VENICE, FESTA DEL REDENTORE (third Saturday of July): The most famous of Venice's celebrations when all the boats become bridges and fireworks light up all the nocturnal revelry.

VERONA, "VERONESE" SUMMER AND OPERA SEASON AT THE ARENA (July-September): Opera festival featuring international star names and performances of dance, theatre and music in the evocative settings of the Arena and the Roman theater.

FELTRE, PALIO (beginning of August): Medieval games, costume parades, races and food fairs re-evoke the entrance of Feltre under the aegis of the Republic of Venice.

VENICE, INTERNATIONAL FILM FESTIVAL (Venice Lido, the end of August): Famous and long-established showcase for all the stars of world cinema.

VENICE, HISTORICAL REGATTA (first Sunday of September): Large regatta on the Grand Canal of antique boats and oarsmen in costume preceded by the splendid historical parade.

MONTAGNANA (first Sunday of September): Historical parade, palio of the "dieci comuni" and horse races in memory of the end of the tyranny of Ezzelino da Romano over the city.

MAROSTICA, THE GAME OF CHESS (in September, every two years): impressive historical game of chess with human figures in costume which takes place in Piazza Castello.

Gathered from the fertile soil and the nearby sea – vegetables, fruit and lots of fish – the people of Veneto, drawing on centuries of know-how, cook their produce according to time-honored recipes and come up with the most delicious dishes.

Food festivals, fairs and culinary delights in Veneto

PROVINCE OF VENICE

PRAMAGGIORE *(March): Festival in celebration of Montasio cheese.*

SCORZÈ *(second week of May): Strawberries and asparagus festival.*

CHIOGGIA *(second week of July): Fish festival.*

PROVINCE OF BELLUNO

LAMON *(September 15-17): White bean festival.*

PROVINCE OF PADUA

CONCHE DI CODEVIGO *(April 22-May 1): Week of the asparagus.*

CALZIGNANO TERME *(May 28): Strawberry festival.*

MASSANZAGO *(July 13-18): Melon Festival.*

ESTE *(the whole of August): Showcase for all the wines of the Euganean vineyards.*

PROVINCE OF ROVIGO

PORTO TOLLE *(July 29-August 6): Fish festival.*

BADIA POLESINE *(September 10-20): Polenta festival.*

PROVINCE OF TREVISO

VAZZOLA VIZNÀ *(March 15-30): Vintage wines festival.*

FARRA DI SOL *(April 24-May 1): Strawberry and asparagus festival.*

SANTANDRA *(May 15-30): Yearly showcase for local cheeses.*

PIEVE DI SOLIGO *(October 1-10) Festival of the giant spit.*

TREVISO AND CASTELFRANCO VENETO *(December 12-20): Showcase and fair for the celebrated red cabbage of Treviso and Castelfranco.*

PROVINCE OF VERONA

SOAVE *(May 21): White wines of Soave festival.*

BARDOLINO *(May): Claret wine festival.*

CAZZANO AND MONTEFORTE *(June 4): Cherry festival and showcase.*

MEZZANE DI SOTTO: *(June 11): Cherry festival.*

TERRAZZO *(September 3): Apple festival.*

SOAVE AND BARDOLINO *(September): Grape and wine festival.*

PROVINCE OF VICENZA

BASSANO DEL GRAPPA *(April 29-30): Showcase for the Bassano asparagus.*

BREGANZE *(May 20-28): Wine festival.*

MAROSTICA *(May 28): Cherry festival.*

BASSANO DEL GRAPPA *(September) Grape festival.*

Spotlight on VENETO'S CELEBRITIES

Veneto: home through the centuries of the great and famous: explorers, musicians, painters, sculptors, playwrights, architects, libertines

Marco Polo (1254-1324). The son of a sea merchant, he travelled with his father to Asia when he was seventeen and ended up staying in the Orient for twenty-four years, most of which time he spent at the court of the Tartars. He returned to Italy in 1295 and, thanks to the intervention of Rustichello of Pisa, published the memoirs of his travels in one of the most widely read books in the world – *Il Milione*.

Aldo Manuzio (1450-1515). Born in Bassano, he was an editor and perhaps the greatest ever Italian typographer. He spent a great deal of his life in Venice, creating the most elegant printing fonts and publishing splendid editions of the classics.
He published works by Homer, Aristotle, Plato and Erasmus. He was also responsible for a superb edition of the *Divine Comedy*.

Titian (1488-1576). Born in Pieve di Cadore (his house can still be visited), he produced a wealth of work in his long lifetime. He was the chief exponent of the Venetian school. His masterpieces still hang in Veneto – in Venice's **Galleria dell'Accademia** and the **church of the Frari** where his superlative *Assumption* rises in the sanctuary.

Giorgione (1478-1510). Born in Castelfranco Veneto, he died young and very little is known of him. He anticipated the luminosity and the emphasis on color which Veneto artists were to so masterfully develop and also invented tonal painting. His masterpieces include the *Tempest* and the *Three Philosophers*. Giorgione opened the great 16th century period of Venetian art.

Ruzante (1496-1542). Originating from Padua, his real name was **Angelo Beolco**. He was one of the first and best dramatists, bringing to the stage the trials and tribulations of the poorer classes in works which were often performed in the local dialect.
His works include *Betia*, the *Musket* and *Fiorina*.

Andrea Palladio (1508-1580). Architect of immense talent and renown, he re-invented old classical architecture, adding harmonious touches of his own which were to spawn a host of imitators. Vicenza was his native city and it's there that his masterpieces can be found and his home can be visited.

Antonio Vivaldi (1678-1741). Known as the "prete rosso" (the red priest) because of his tawny hair, he is among the best composers and musicians of all time. He bequeathed to the world more than five hundred musical scores including operas, concertos and sonnets. For many years he was the music maestro in the **church of Santa Maria della Pietà** in Venice.

Carlo Goldoni (1707-1793). Originating from Venice, he is the greatest Italian comedy dramatist. He transformed the Commedia dell'arte into a comedy of humors with real characters. His works include *The Landlady*, *Arlecchino, Server of Two Masters* and *The Campiello*. There's a museum dedicated to him in Venice in **Palazzo Centani**.

Lorenzo da Ponte (1749-1838). Born in Cènada, now Vittorio Veneto, he was a Jew who later converted to Christianity (his real name was **Emanuele Conegliano**) and who became the great librettist of Mozart's operas, including *The Marriage of Figaro*, *Don Giovanni* and *Così fan tutte*.

Giacomo Casanova (1725-1798). The Venetian Casanova was the prototype of the libertine who broke every moral rule. Travelling all over Europe, he was imprisoned several times but succeeded in breaking free, in a famous escape, even from the Piombi prison in Venice. In the dungeons of **Palazzo Ducale** one can still today visit his cell.

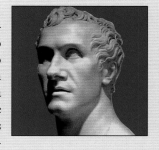

Antonio Canova (1757-1822). Born in Possagno where one may pay a visit to the **Gipsoteca**, the museum containing his casts, Canova was the greatest sculptor of the neo-classical period and his work was sought after and acclaimed in the whole of Europe. He worked for popes and emperors and executed a portrait of Napoleon and his family. His work is renowned for its harmony and grace.

Contemporary artists and writers from Veneto

The great Veneto tradition, renowned for its informed sensibility and psychological insight, continues to produce distinguished artists. Besides the excellent sculptor Arturo Martini *(one of his works is featured in the photo) and the gifted poet* Andrea Zanzotto, *there are many talented writers including* Guido Piovene *and* Goffredo Parise, *both of whom are excellent journalists, the sunny* Giovanni Comisso, *the surreal* Dino Buzzati *and the interesting trio made up of* Sgorlon, Saviane *and* Cibotto.

Apart from various universal geniuses like Giorgione, Titian, Palladio *and* Canova, *other distinguished artists especially in the figurative field who have contributed to the great artistic heritage of Veneto are featured in the report on Veneto Art.*

More than 20 centuries of art
from Roman mosaics to the dominion of Verona until Venice bursts upon the scene

Prehistory and the masterpieces of the Romans

Though there exist collections of Veneto art dating back to the 6th century BC (small bronze statues, modelled glass) created by the indigenous populations and the Illyrian culture, it's with the advent of the Romans that Veneto's artistic heritage truly begins to avail itself of a significant body of artistic treasures, especially in cities like Aquileia, Caorle and Padua. Proof of this is supplied by the mosaics in Aquileia's and Verona's basilicas, by the Roman *Gavi* and *Borsari* arches and, above all, by the splendidly preserved **Arena** in Verona.

From the barbarians to San Zeno

The centuries of the barbarian invasions then followed. Veneto was under threat from Byzantine Ravenna, from the East and from Longobard Lombardy: a wealth of cultures which were to enrich the cultural heritage of the area. One thinks of the bronze doors of Verona's San Zeno – a masterpiece of Othonian sculpture – and the city's stupendous **Cathedral**. It was Verona in fact, rather than Venice, which in the period around 1000 held a monopoly of the arts in Veneto despite the small architectural gems constituted by such parish churches as the **Bardolino** or **San Giorgio in Valpollicella**.

Art in Veneto, from the Comuni to the Signorie
The splendor of the Scaligere Tombs

With the rise of the Signorie – powerful families like the Carraresi in Padua and the Scaligeri in Verona – powerful new expressive forms were to emerge in architecture. The *Arche Scaligere* and the *Monument to Cangrande* in Verona pay testament to these developments. In Padua, the **Palazzo della Ragione** emerged and in Treviso the stunning **Loggia dei Cavalieri**. Then, at the beginning of the 14th century, and remaining something of an isolated phenomenon, Padua's *Cappella degli Scrovegni* was raised with its stunning cycle of frescoes by **Giotto**. In his thirty nine scenes from the *Life of Jesus*, Giotto ensured that Italian art was to take a giant step forward and these frescoes perhaps represent the birth of modern painting.

When Venice appears on the scene

In the meantime, the young Venice appeared on the artistic scene thanks initially to **Torcello** where one can see the mosaic of the *Last Judgement* and immediately chose as its stylistic characteristic the use of color which was to make the Venetian school unique in the history of art. Beginning in the 1200s, a great center of activity for Venetian artists was provided by the **Basilica di San Marco**. Various groups of artists and artisans were to enrich the basilica with a variety of successive styles, ranging from the Romanesque to the Byzantine influences arriving by sea from the East and from nearby Ravenna. Already, in the Basilica's early mosaics, the dazzling nature of the colors reigns supreme, which is especially the case regarding those that decorate the narthex. The building is steeped in influences from the East – with which Venice maintained close and friendly trading links – and the forms, right down to the glittering domes, pay heady testament to this fact.

THE CHURCHES OF TORCELLO, PAOLO VENEZIANO AND THE ARTISTIC INFLUENCE OF RAVENNA

Venice found its Giotto in **Paolo Veneziano**, a worthy artist who, through the course of his career, was to evolve his painting style. He begun very much under Byzantine influences only to become more Gothicly-orientated as can be seen in his work: *La Madonna della Galleria* in Venice, the *Death of the Virgin* in Vicenza and the *Crowning of Mary* again in Venice.

The great high Gothic period

By the end of the 1300s, Venice, having benefited from the lesson bestowed by Byzantine decorative art, was among the first cities in Italy to embrace and develop the artistic style known now as the high Gothic. Refined decoration and a structural lightness in architecture gave birth to masterpieces such as the Ca' d'Oro *(Palazzo Contarini), the* Palazzo Ducale *(which took an entire century to build) and the* Basilica di Santa Maria dei Frari. *It was around this time that* Palazzo Ducale's *lavish windows were created and the iconostasis in the* Basilica di San Marco *was decorated. The Venice that today casts such a compelling and bewitching spell over everyone who visits it was beginning to take shape. On the other hand, work carried out by great artists such as* Pisanello *and* Gentile da Fabriano, *who during that period lent their skills to the decoration of the Palazzo Ducale, has vanished without trace, never to be seen.*

More than 20 centuries of art
When Venetian colorism paved
the way for western painting

Venetian quattrocento: from Bellini to Carpaccio

It was an artist from Sicily, **Antonello da Messina**, who, by making the switch from Venetian tempera painting to the greater lucidity and attention to detail of oil painting, was to revolutionize Veneto art. The **Bellini** family immediately fell under his influence and the masterpieces of **Giovanni Bellini** can be found in the *Sala di Maggior Consiglio* of **Palazzo Ducale** and in the famous *Pala di Giobbe*. One of Bellini's pupils was **Vittorio Carpaccio** who excelled in painting large compositional paintings full of figures (**Scuola di Sant'Orsola** and **San Giorgio degli Schiavoni** in Venice).

Carpaccio: the Miraculous Healing of a Madman *(detail)*.

The golden century of Giorgione and Titian

The Quattro and Cinquecento saw the rise of two of western art's great geniuses, **Giorgione** and then his pupil, **Titian**. These two painters were to initiate a revolutionary painting style founded on a use of color which allowed an atmospheric transparency and vibrancy. Giorgione's masterpieces include the *Philosophers*, *Venus* and the *Tempest*. Titian, originating from Pieve di Cadore, was then to display his unrivalled genius throughout the sixteenth century and his figurative compositions displayed both a pathos and sensuality which are still breathtaking to behold. His innovative use of color has given him the title of prince of Venetian painting and his supreme masterpiece is the *Assumption* in the **Chiesa dei Frari**.

The masters of Mannerism, followed by Palladio

Half way through the sixteenth century mannerism began making its impact on Veneto art and found its richest expression in the work of artists like Jacopo Tintoretto, Bassano *and* Veronese. *Tintoretto's splendid handling of space to create great dramatic tension and emotion can be admired in his works on display in the* Scuola di San Rocco. *The driving concern of Jacopo da Bassano, on the other hand, was to restore beauty to nature with a great expressive force which he did so successfully. And finally, there's Veronese who in his paintings reflects the joy of living in Venice in the 16th century. His frescoes in the* Villa Barbaro-Maser *perhaps represent his finest achievement.*

At the same time, Venice, but above all Vicenza and the entire Veneto region were benefitting from the genial architecture of Palladio *whose re-elaboration of classical values was to find its best expression in the many villas he designed in the area.*

Imagination and irony in the Tiepolo family

The great tradition of 16th century fresco painting begun by Veronese was taken up by **Giambattista Tiepolo** whose work, in the 18th century, was sought after throughout Europe. His ambitious, ingeniously-composed mythological and heroic frescoes were to grace the walls of palaces, villas and churches throughout the Veneto region. A feature on his work in the region can be found in the Vicenza part of this guide. His frescoes in **Villa Pisani**, near Padua deserve a special mention. His son **Giandomenico**, on the other hand, was to continue the fresco tradition in a lighter, more ironic tone whose style sometimes verged on the point of caricature. A direct comparison of the two different styles can be found in the **Villa Valmarana ai Nani** in Vicenza where the work of father and son sit side by side.

Francesco Guardi: The island of San Giorgio *(detail)*.

The splendid art of the vedutisti

Eighteenth century art in Venice is famous for the style of landscape painting known as "vedutismo" which had in **Bellotto** and **Canaletto** two of its supreme interpreters. Bellotto painted a series of haunting landscapes of Venice as a young man before moving to northern Europe where he was to enjoy tremendous fame and fortune. Canaletto has bequeathed us a series of limpid and luminous views of Venice in which the city's monuments and landscapes are depicted with a loving attention to detail. The work of **Francesco Guardi** is very different. He captures the melancholy of a decadent and disordered Venice, no longer suffused by soft limpid light but at the mercy of both harsher and dirtier colors and atmospheric techniques. Also worth mentioning as a chronicler of Venice is the painter of interiors **Pietro Longhi** who has left us with a vibrant and detailed set of studies of life in Venice's salons and theaters.

The solitary genius of Canova

When the Republic fell and Venice was seized first by the French and then by the Austrians, the art and expressive life of the city went into decline. The only Veneto artist of note in the 19th century was the sculptor Antonio Canova. *The artist who sculpted the* bust of Napoleon *and his family was the principle and most original purveyor of the neoclassical style which marked a return to the ideal of beauty held in classical times. For the grace of his forms, the harmony of his figures and groups, the smooth flow of his lines in the marble, Canova remains a unique artist in the history of art. Canova's work can be admired in the* Gipsoteca *in his native town of Possagno, near Treviso, where casts of all his major works are collected.*

Spotlight on VENETO VILLAS

Scattered throughout the cities and countryside of Veneto, the almost three thousand Veneto villas, recently restored and now open to the public, are a heritage unique to the region

The villa, a palace in the countryside

The villa came into being for a variety of reasons: financial gain, social prestige, the need for physical and spiritual well-being. These splendid country homes built by the Veneto nobility were often designed by the best architects of their day and reached their aesthetic peak with the many works by the great Palladio. Stunning in appearance, these villas were also fitted out with all the interior comforts of the time and often lavishly decorated with frescoes, stuccos and wrought iron. The great Veneto families were determined that their country homes be no less lavish and impressive than their town houses. The scope of the villa was also to allow the landlords to preside over the agricultural work in the fields and vineyards, the tending of the livestock and the general upkeep and cultivation of the land. The villa also, of course, provided a country retreat where these powerful families could relax among friends and enjoy the spiritual benefits of the countryside.

Fruit of the 15th century

The Veneto villa first saw the light in the 1400s and its steady proliferation and use continued until the end of the 18th century when the Republic fell and the region's golden age came to an end. The villa was a phenomenon which occurred principally in the countryside throughout the whole region but above all in the provinces of Vicenza and Verona. In the 15th century villas also began to appear on the islands of the lagoon.

These villas, of which there are such an abundant and splendidly eclectic number, are graced with a variety of architectural styles though, for the most part, bear the hallmark of Gothic or Renaissance design.

The planning of the Veneto villa

Two construction plans prevailed where the Veneto villa was concerned. The first entailed a villa with an adjacent tower graced with an elegant portico and a loggia above. The second entailed a villa which was covered by two sloping roofs and graced by windows with one light. Often the styles employed in these villas derived from the palaces in the cities but the orientation of the country villas was always carefully planned to allow the maximum influx of sunlight and to make sure the building enjoyed a harmonious relationship with the surrounding countryside.

When commerce with the Orient began to wane, the Venetian nobility turned their attention inwards: the great period of the Veneto villas

With the advent of the 16th century, the villa is no longer an isolated building; stables, barns, haylofts and towers for breeding pigeons begin to appear

Palladio, the genius of the Veneto villa

The leading light behind the innovation of the concept of the villa was, without question, the great Veneto architect Andrea Palladio *(1508-1580) who magisterially unified and blended an architectural style which was both functional and aesthetically pleasing to the eye. His style, introducing elegant porticos and facades which bore the look of temples, was rigorously classical and in its pleasing visual harmonies often surpassed the grandeur of the city palaces themselves.*

Among the masterpieces of this great architect we can mention here only a few – Villa Barbaro in Maser, *near Treviso,* Villa Emo Capodilista, *near Rovigo and, above all, the supremely beautiful* Rotonda *on the outskirts of Vicenza.*

The villas of the 17th and 18th centuries

Veneto in the 17th century underwent a series of calamities – wars, famines and plagues – which meant that the construction of elegant villas fell into decline, at least during the first half of the century. The second half though saw the emergence of some fine architects among whom Baldassarre Longhena *and* Antonio Pizzocaro. *The 18th century however witnessed a revival in Venice and Veneto's fortunes and with it a new demand for sumptuous homes. Once again a new array of stately villas began gracing the countryside. Often these were adorned with family chapels, large stables and luxurious guest quarters. The interiors of these villas would be adorned with frescoes, stuccos, statues while the gardens*

too were elaborately conceived to include fountains, statuary, ornamental lakes and groves. Often they were built in the style of Palladio *with the pronaos surmounted by a triangular pediment.*

Spotlight on CONVENTS, HERMITAGES AND SANCTUARIES

In sacred Veneto, among cloisters, masterpieces and herb gardens

Lavishly endowed with centuries-old convents, abbeys and sanctuaries, Veneto reveals its history and religious faith not only to tourists but also to pilgrims of the faith. Here are a few itineraries for those eager to discover cloisters, works of art and old herbalist products including natural medicines which one can purchase from the monks

Venice: The Abbey of San Giorgio Maggiore. On the island of San Giorgio, now the home of the Giorgio Cini Foundation, rises the great abbey built in 982 by the first abbot, **Giovanni Morosini**. Ever since then the Benedictine monks have enjoyed an unbroken stay there. The **Basilica** is splendid, executed by **Palladio** and contains celebrated works by **Tintoretto**. The wooden *crucifix* attributed to **Brunelleschi** is stupendous. Here one can buy the excellent honey from the hives in the gardens on the island.
Venice: Convent of San Francesco del

Deserto. In 1228 a small church was built on the small island near Burano, where St Francis of Assisi wanted to land. After two centuries of sitting abandoned, it was enlarged in 1451. It has always been the domain of the Franciscan monks. It is set in a stunning natural environment. The **Chiesa delle Stimmate** is austere and the *cloister*, built in 1100, is admirable for its simplicity. It is open to group tours or one can pass a few nights here in order to engage in spiritu al reflection.
Follina (Treviso): Abbazia Santuario di Santa Maria. Located in a beautiful me-

dieval village, near Conegliano, this abbey which is more than a thousand years old, first of all belonged to the Benedictines, then the Cistercians, before passing into the hands of the Camaldolites and finally, in the 1900s, the servants of Mary. The **Basilica** is the object of many pilgrimages and possesses elements of both Romanesque and Gothic styles. It also houses the stone statue of the *Blessed Virgin of Follina*. The *cloister*, *sacristy* and *refectory* are all impressive. The abbey also hosts concerts and is open to guests.

Oriental spirituality, from sacred icons to rose jam

Monastero dell'Isola degli Armeni

In the1700s a group of Armenian Mekhitarist fathers founded this spiritual center, which still thrives today, on one of Venice's small islands, the old leper colony of San Lazzaro. The Romanesque and Gothic church was built in the 14th century; the *cloisters* and remaining buildings all date back to the 1700s. There's a fine museum containing artifacts from Armenian and oriental antiquity and a library endowed with a fresco by **Giambattista Tiepolo**. The ceremonies of Armenian ritual, including the Sunday Mass, are open to the public and well worth observing. There's also a printing press which serves the Armenian community. And don't leave without buying a jar of the excellent *rose jam* which the fathers produce from the roses in their gardens.

The Abbey of Praglia

Twelve kilometers from Abano Terme, at the foot of the Euganean hills in the vicinity of Praglia, can be found the **Abbey of Santa Maria Assunta**, a national monument. It comprises of a **basilica**, four *cloisters* (ranging in origin from Gothic to Renaissance). It also possesses an engaging *refectory* and *library* with more than 100,000 volumes. Honey, Apis Euganean cream and liquors – Amaro, Medical Grahem, China – can be brought, all made with herbs grown in the convent.

The apothecaries

Abano Terme: Sanctuary of Santa Maria di Monteortone. Perched on a wooded hill of oaks and chestnuts where, it's said, a miraculous image of the Madonna was found, rises this temple designed by **Pietro** and **Tulio Lombardo**. The three-aisled interior contains important frescoes by the 15th century artist **Jacopo da Montagnana** which unfortunately are now badly damaged. There are also fine bas-reliefs depicting *God the Father and Prophets*. In a small *chapel* can be found the sacred image depicting the *Virgin with Child*. Beside the sanctuary, there's the **Monastery** belonging to the Augustine monks.

Bardolino (Verona): hermitage of Monte San Giorgio. Near the hamlet of San Vito, one climbs a rock to this 17th century Camaldolite hermitage which commands a sweeping view over Lake Garda. The **church of San Giorgio** stands on a small square and contains a splendid work of art: the *San Romualdo* painted by **Palma il Giovane**. There are also eight secluded cells and a vegetable garden. The hermitage will accept guests.

Verona: Convento santuario di Santa Teresa del Bambino Gesù. Erected at the beginning of the century, neo-Gothic in style and dedicated to Santa Francese, this convent contains many fine frescoes, statues, paintings and decorations. A weekly organ concert is open to the general public and one can also stay for lunch. *Acqua di Melissa*, produced and sold by the Carmelite monks, enjoys great fame; it has been around since the 1700s, consists of oils distilled in alcohol and is a remedy for many ailments including stomach disorders and migraine. The sanctuary's shop is, in fact, always bustling with trade.

Other important sanctuaries: anyone wanting to get to know the most alluring sanctuaries of Veneto should certainly not ignore two great pilgrimage sites – in Vicenza, the **Santuario della Beata Vergine di Monte Berico** and in Padua, the **Basilica del Santo** (Sant'Antonio) around which revolves the tourist trade of the entire city. Both of these religious retreats will be reviewed later, in the chapters on Vicenza and Padua respectively.

Every old Italian convent possessed an almshouse for the poor, a hospice and often a herb garden. From the latter, the expert monks would extract herbs and plants which they distilled and made into medicinal remedies or liquors. A tour of the surviving monastery apothecaries makes for a fascinating experience. All the items produced by the monks are of course 100% natural and as such in great demand. Today, the monks are above all distillers of liquors and herbs and creators of natural medicinal and cosmetic products like perfumes and creams. Also well-worth sampling are the delicious jams (for example, the rose jam) and the honey, collected from the convent hives. A visit to these tranquil and often isolated religious retreats offers a rare spiritual reprieve from the hustle and bustle of the modern world as well as perhaps providing a treat for your taste buds or a cure for some nagging ailment.

Sanctuary of the Madonna del Pilastrello. Near Rovigo, in Lendinara, can be found this impressive 16th century sanctuary which stands next to a monastery. The sanctuary contains an image of the Madonna, held to be endowed with miraculous powers – a faithful copy of the original small wooden statue which was stolen in recent times. Here, in this serene monastic atmosphere, two paintings of note can also be admired – the *Ascension* by Paolo Veronese and a *Saint Francis* by Piazzetta. Water believed to possess healing powers runs through the Cappella del Bagno.

A trip to the Veneto parks: from the Dolomites to the Po

From the woods and the snow of the Dolomites around Ampezzo and Belluno to the Euganean natural springs, the museums of the Lessini heights and the spellbinding river Sile

From the mountains to the lagoons

Besides being a depository of illustrious art and history, Veneto is also a paradise for excursionists and nature lovers thanks to the five large nature reserves, all of which have been created by the region or the state in recent times. A concise guide is offered here which will help the tourist or sightseer to make the most of the impressive wonders of nature to be found in these parks, wonders which take many forms including, from the Dolomites in the north to the big river *Po* in the south, mountainous valleys, picturesque hills, natural springs, woods and rivers. Landscapes often distinguished by beauty spots or the presence of a particular flora and fauna. The lover of nature will be able to observe both indigenous and migratory birds in the warmth of the lagoons, fossils preserved in the rocks and all manner of rare plants, including lakeside and Alpine varieties.

The Ampezzo Dolomites Nature Reserve

Run by the "Comunanza delle Regole d'Ampezzo" (a syndicate of old local families), the park (11,200 hectares) is situated in a vast protected area amounting in total to over 37,000 hectares in the municipality of Cortina – the heart of the eastern Dolomites. A severe and majestic landscape though varied, ranging from the low valleys to the sylvan pine and larch woods, the manifold fields, the rocky heights and the snowfields. It also incorporates various mountain ranges, including the *Tofana* whose summit exceeds 3,200 metres.

The Euganean hills Nature Reserve

Not far from Padua, we find the first regional park created in Veneto (1989): it covers 18,000 hectares and incorporates the chief hilly area of the Pianura Padana (as many as 81 hills, the tallest of which is 601 metres). Agriculture and tourism are the mainstays of this splendid place which has been inhabited since prehistoric times. Olive groves, vineyards and fruit orchards are cultivated in an eco-friendly fashion. There are thick and flourishing chestnut, oak and hornbeam groves as well as the remains of medieval castles.

The Lessinia Nature Reserve

Not far from Verona, the Lessini Nature Reserve is a large plateau which stretches from the slopes of the Adige valley to the foot of the Small Dolomites. Created in 1990, it combines pasturing fields with thick woods. Its characteristics include the remains of the spontaneous architecture of the old Cimbri population and the natural karstic erosion. The zone is richly endowed with museums documenting the natural, historical and human characteristics of the Lessini heights.

The Sile River Nature Reserve

In the Treviso area, this park on water and for water, follows and documents, between swamps and medieval architecture, the environment of the river *Sile* (almost 100 Km long) which is the longest resurgent river in Europe. There is the *Parco Alto* (the high park), the *Urban Park*, in the area of Treviso and, finally, the *Archaeological Park of Quarto* di Altino.
Fountains, lakes, swamp areas, small watercourses and a rich fauna constitute an environment also inhabited by falcons, buzzards and herons.

The Nature Reserve of the Belluno Dolomites

This National Park, located between Belluno, Agordo and Feltre, is, in many ways, the other side of the Dolomites where tourists and nature lovers will come face to face with woods and meadows, canyons and silent valleys, pinnacles and steep cliffs in an expanse of terrain extending to more than 30,00 hectares. The park is also a joy to naturalists because of the more than fifty types of falcon it provides a sanctuary for, as well as the lime, fir, birch and maple woods. All kinds of flowers can be found here too, including, in the higher realms, edelweiss and saxifrage. Deer, chamois, roe bucks as well as martens and

ermines all live here. The eagle and the owl build their nests here and you're also likely to catch a glimpse of the capercaillie and the white partridge.
Traces of communication trenches from the First World War have also survived which can be seen in the area.

The dinosaurs of Bussolengo (Verona)

Located eighteen kilometres from Verona, not far from Lake Garda, we find the Natura Viva Park *(40,000 mq), a vegetable and faunistic oasis where, among the lush greenery and the spring water, more than 690 species of rare or almost-extinct animals are gathered.*
The park boasts two options: there's a safari park where a car is obligatory and then the true wildlife park where you'll also come across a unique Dinosaur Park *in which these animals have been recreated life size in fiberglass. A paradise for naturalists and lovers of nature.*

The spellbinding lagoon of Averto

Along the Romea road, not far from Chioggia, lavishes a typical fishing valley extending for more than 500 hectares which for a dozen or so years has been protected by the W.W.F. as an "oasis for the protection of wildlife". A wealth of poplars, alders, oaks and ashes surround expanses of sea water inhabited by various species of fish among the reeds and canals and varied vegetation which includes rushes and waterlillies. Among the numerous species of birds which make their nests in this oasis we find the mallard, the pintail duck, the red heron together with swans that co-exist with hawks and ospreys. This splendid oasis in the Averto valley is open to visitors every day. For further information contact: W.W.F. Italia, Tel. 041/5185068.

The yellow gold of the poor

*For years polenta has kept hunger at bay in Italy,
today it is a refined dish for the connoisseurs of good food
and Veneto is its home*

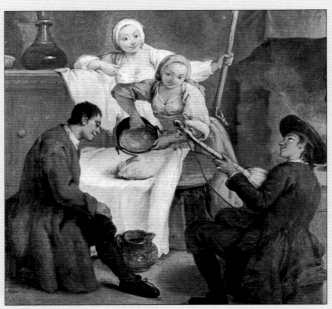

Polenta, a lunch and a legend: since the 1500s – in other words, for five centuries – polenta has been the staple diet of the poor in Italy and especially in Veneto. Recent prosperity and the end of the peasant culture have transformed the identity of polenta which, though remaining very popular in this region, has now become something of a simple but refined dish suitable for the connoisseur of fine food.

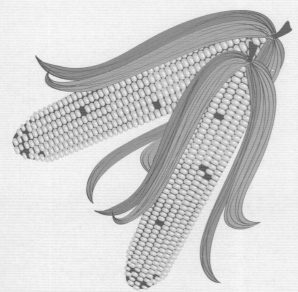

From the Americas arrives maize

The advent of maize flour took place with the discovery of America and Veneto immediately took advantage of the new ingredient. Thirty years later the first harvests of maize appeared, but it wasn't until the 1600s that maize was cultivated on a large scale though the Venetian, Giambattista Ramusio already alludes to fields of maize in Veneto in 1554. At the beginning of the 1600s the yellow flour was used in Venice to make bread. Soon it was to replace millet as the chief ingredient of polenta on the tables of the poor. However, at the beginning of the 1700s, maize was found to cause the illness called pelegra which is a serious form of avitaminosis.

The long history of polenta

Polenta features in a classic of world literature, **Goldoni**'s *La donna di garbo* when, in the long and brilliant monologue, Rosaura relates to Arlecchino how one should cook and prepare the maize-based dish. On the facing page one can admire a splendid portrait of the genre by Pietro Longhi, who was more or less a contemporary of Goldoni. These are two examples of how polenta is much more than a simple meal but rather a veritable cultural symbol for the working class population of Veneto. Polenta was an integral means of filling hungry bellies in every poor household. It was cooked in a copper pot over the embers of the stove and when ready, poured into the large round serving dish and eaten in company. Once upon a time polenta was known by the name, "ammazzafame" (hunger-killer); now however it is referred to as "sole nel piatto" (sun on a plate).

The Romans ate polenta, though in those days it was made with other flours; afterwards it became the staple diet of the pre-Columbian populations. For five centuries polenta has been the native dish of Veneto.

A world of symbols

The symbolical meanings linked to maize and polenta are numerous. In Veneto homes it was a custom to leave hanging in the kitchen a bunch of corncobs as a token of fertility and good fortune. There are also several erotically-flavored allusions attributed to it, once more tied up with the notion of fertility. Thus, the long ladle which is used to stir the polenta in the pan represents the union between man and woman. It's an insult to call a young person a **scartosso** *– the leaf of the maize which was used to stuff the mattresses of the poor.*

A hundred ways to prepare polenta

It would be impossible to list all the possible ways of preparing polenta and utilizing it with other ingredients. It can be served soft or toasted, a tocheti (cold and cut into pieces) or made with bacon; alternatively, it can be fried (with egg and breadcrumbs). Then there's polenta al montasio (sprinkled with monta-sio cheese cut into slices); polenta pastissada – cooked with small pieces of meat, garlic and onion. Polenta can be served up with many other ingredients – for example with baccalà or lugànega, or else with milk, cooked herbs or beans. The most authentic and traditional polenta though is simply sliced and served hot from the chopping board.

Spotlight on FISH

Sea and fresh water fish in Veneto

A cuisine based on a hundred variations, from trout to baccalà and shellfish but which employs simple cooking methods and natural seasoning

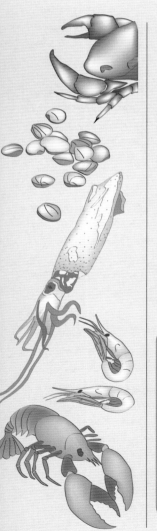

Both refined and simple, Veneto cuisine is based largely on seafood, so much so that the most representative dish is *fish risotto*, which comes in a variety of forms (with seafood, scampi, eel, cuttlefish). Another local speciality are the small fried fish which can be brought from the *fritolani* (fish stalls on the street) and eaten with polenta.

A very longstanding tradition where Veneto is concerned, fish was once salted and marinated in order to conserve it for long periods before eating. The methods of cooking fish, though enriched by dozens of creative variations, have however remained rooted to a few simple procedures – boiling, frying, grilling and oven cooking. The seasonings used are also simple but tasty: olive oil, vinegar, parsley, garlic and spiced herbs. There are of course specific recipes regarding the infinite variety of shellfish available to the Veneto kitchen. Veneto has a fine tradition regarding both sea fish and fresh water fish, which is especially the case with the delicious trout to be found in Treviso.

Shellfish

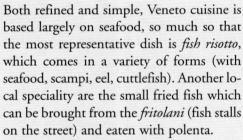

Shellfish reign supreme all along the Adriatic coast, cooked, as for example in Chioggia, in a casso pipa – an earthenware saucepan – boiled slowly (pipar in Venetian dialect) and perhaps served in white wine. In Caorle, the soups and brodetti are famous and of course served together with polenta. Especially recommended where the cephaloped variety of fish are concerned are the dormouse, cuttlefish, squid and octopus. As for shellfish, lobster makes for a delicious dish and is a speciality of Sile in the Treviso region thanks to the quality of its red lobsters.

"El bacalà alla vicentina"

Pride of place of Veneto cuisine goes to the famous bacalà alla vicentina *which, the cod cooked over a low flame with garlic, onion, olive oil, milk and parmesan cheese, becomes a delicate dish as much at home in the elegant stylish restaurant as a rustic trattoria. Traditionally Venetian, there's also* bacalà mantecato *in which the softened dried cod is cooked in olive oil, salt, pepper, parsley and garlic, then creamed in a blender and served tepid or cold on slices of polenta. Excellent also are* bacalà frito, bacalà alla trevisana *and* bacalà al pomodoro *which is kept soaked for twenty four hours, doused in onion and herbs browned in oil and cooked in a tomato sauce for three hours. In Veneto bacalé is almost always served with polenta.*

Cooking fish with flair

From the seafood hors d'oeuvre to the celebrated risottos;
from "sardine in saor" to boiled eel, from fresh water fish to frogs

Now and again in this report we have mentioned a series of fish dishes typical of the Veneto region. First and foremost, it is the various risottos which dominate the Veneto menus. *Risotto alla seppie* is a favorite dish and a bright black color as a result of the cuttlefish being cooked in its own ink. Another classic Venetian starter is the *brodetto di pesce* (fish soup) which is particularly delicious when spiced with saffron.

Perhaps not the lightest of meals, but nevertheless very popular is the *zuppa di cozze* (mussel soup) which, in Veneto, is prepared with garlic, parsley and a little white wine. Spaghetti with fresh clams cooked in a spicy sauce of red peppers is another local speciality.

To begin your meal on the right foot, a starter of seafood is always a safe bet – lobster, mussels, crab,

squid etc – served up with olive oil and lemon. If, in Veneto cuisine, salame, duck and game all enjoy great popularity, it is still fish which rules the roost even where second courses are concerned. Among the most tasty and simple dishes, there's *sardine in saor* (marinated sardines), or *anguille in umido* – boiled eels, cooked in a tomato sauce with garlic and white wine.

Though the entire region is within easy reach of the sea, Veneto cuisine also makes great use of fresh water fish, especially popular are carp, pike, the small roach, goby, rudd, chub, which is found in the streams of the pianura, tench, trout and then crawfish, eels and frogs which are safeguarded by a regional law in March and April and during the night when it is forbidden to catch them.

Fresh water trout is a great favorite in Veneto. It features in many local recipes, including the *risòto con la truta* which is served cooked in wine, salt and pepper, *trute in graèla*, grilled trout served in butter with parsley and celery, *trute in saor*, trout cooked in white wine, vinegar, nutmeg, ginger and cloves. There's also *trute nel forno* (baked trout) and *trute fumegade* (smoked trout).

From trout we move onto eels, for which Sile in the Treviso area is particularly renowned. In Veneto eels are called *buratelli* if they weight less than a hundred and fifty grams, *scarezzoni*, if they weigh up to half a kilo and *bisàte* if they are heavier. Eels are extremely nourishing – containing both protein and fat – but very easy to digest. Once again Veneto has come up with a vast array of recipes which bring out the best in eels, including *bisàta in saor*, *risòto con la bisàta* or *in graèla*. Eels are also cooked in a baking dish in foil and served with polenta which constitutes a traditional lunch on Holy Saturday.

A delight which has endured 500 years

The great cheeses of the Veneto region

Fertile with its plains, valleys and mountains, Veneto reaps from its vigorous livestock a copious supply of milk which in turn, drawing on more than a thousand years of tradition, is made into a number of excellent cheeses, some of which we here invite you to sample

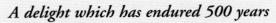

A history of cheese

Cheese was probably born in late palaelolithic times when man first began domesticating animals. For centuries however cheese was to be made only from goats and sheep milk. In the British Museum in London there's the "dairy frieze", a famous Sumerian bas-relief. When cheese passed from Greece to Rome it became a veritable industry: it's featured in the "rations of the legionnaire" where it's eaten smoked. With the successive barbarian invasions cows' milk too finally came to be used for cheese. In the meantime, the growth of

*ASIAGO is alpine produced but prevalent also in Venice. It's protected by the Denominazione di Origine Controllata (the Italian food certification) and is best represented by the *Asiago d'Allevo* (on the mature side) and the *Asiago Pressato* (fresh and sweet). Established since the 1500s, it is produced in both the Vicenza and Treviso regions (160,000 quintals a year). A variety with a stronger flavor is the *Vezzena*.

*CASATELLA, a cheese of a soft texture which has to be eaten fresh within a matter of days and is typical of the Treviso region. It has been a staple part of the diet of countryfolk for centuries.

*MONTASIO, retains the aroma of the flocks and fields and is processed soft. There are three kinds: da tavola, which is matured for two months, mezzano which is more mature and vecchio which is suitable for grating. It's certified by the Origine Controllata and produced in the Treviso region, Belluno, Padua and Venice.

*GRANA PADANO, is a cheese known throughout the world and can be eaten as its found or grated over pasta and other first courses.

Other excellent cheeses from Veneto worth trying include *Provolone*, *Fontal* and *Latteria Piave*.

How cheese is made

Cheese has been made in the same way for five thousand years. It's nothing but curdled milk (from cows, sheep, goats or buffaloes) from which the whey has been extracted. The milk is made to clot thanks to the rennet (extracted from the stomach of the suckling animals). The curdled milk, stirred with wooden or metal spatulas, is put in large sacks to be cleansed of its fats, set into forms and pressed. In this way the whey is separated from the cheese (thanks to which ricotta is made). The cheese is then salted, in order to form the rind and give more flavor. Some cheeses are then left to mature. Thus cheese is made and every region of Italy produces its own variations all of which have a different and distinctive taste.

Cheese,
White bread
And pure wine
Make the heart
stronger

(Veneto proverb)

CHEESE
With polenta, with vine and with pears

In Italy, cheese is generally eaten after the second course, before the dessert or used to add flavor to certain dishes, in particular, pasta. Cheese also forms part of many delicious partnerships.

In Veneto, the traditional companion to cheese is polenta: the most suitable cheeses being *gorgonzola*, *taleggio* and *camembert*; together with *fontina*.

The coupling of wine with pears is legendary to the extent of inspiring proverbs, but other fruits too have been combined with cheese with great success including apricots, cherries and oranges.

The fig makes a fine partner for salted cheeses while *provolone* and *taleggio* bring out the best in melons.

Getting the mix right between wine and cheese is important to the success of any table. Where fresh cheeses are concerned white wine, rosy or young wines are advised.

Brie and camembert harmonize well with full-bodied wines.

Fatty cheeses should be served with fruity white wine or strong red wine. The hard mature cheeses should be accompanied by old vintage red wines.

monarchism brought about the institution of the cheese dairies which were equipped with ingenious devices and instruments invented specifically for the preparation of cheese. 1477 was a pivotal date in the history of cheese – a doctor from the Piemonte area published the first study of cheese, the Summa laticiniorum which, among other things, lists all the different kinds of Italian cheeses of the period, among which we find Marzolino, Robiole and Fontina. The production and consumption of cheese has continued up until the present day and shows no signs of waning in popularity. After all, it's nutritious and tasty and deserves its place on tables throughout the world.

The land of Cockaigne

Cheese, recommended since antiquity by the Medical School of Salernitana as a healthy part of any diet and occupying an integral place on the tables of rich and poor alike, is synonymous with prosperity and riches in the popular imagination of Italy. It's no coincidence that in the etchings and stories of the legendary land of Cockaigne (mythical utopia of idleness and luxury for the poor throughout history) mountains in the forms of cheese, immense heaps of ricotta, other mountains covered in grated cheese and even walls made of parmesan cheese overlook wide lakes of butter. Milk and its products, an essential element in the lives of the poor throughout history, are thus, for the Italian, symbols of beneficence and nutritious prosperity.

Spotlight on THE COFFEE

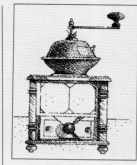

From Islamic brew to espresso

Coffee originated in the East in the 14th century when the Arabs discovered how to roast coffee beans and "invented" the dark-colored liquid known as "Islamic brew". The first coffee-houses were opened in Constantinople in 1554. Coffee reached Italy via Turkish merchant ships. In 1720, during the Enlightenment, when the Caffe alla Venezia Triofante was inaugurated in Venice, coffee represented intellectual vigor and a modern outlook – as opposed to chocolate, which was the old-fashioned drink of the aristocratic classes. It comes as no surprise that Venice is considered the patron of coffee in Italy – one only has to think of two splendid historical coffee-houses in Saint Mark's Square – il **Quadri** and il **Florian**. And from Venice coffee was to spread throughout Italy.

A tour of the most celebrated cafés in Veneto

Successors to the illustrious Viennese café society of the 17 and 18th century when Veneto was part of Austria, cafés steeped in history catch the eye and imagination for their elegant décor and long tradition in Venice, Padua and Verona

IN VENICE

In Saint Mark's square there are two historical cafés of world renown: the Florian and the Quadri. The tourist will be caught in two minds – whether to sit outside and enjoy the colorful activity of the square or settle down inside amidst the elegant splendour of their interiors which are often embellished by the presence of an orchestra. Founded way back in 1720, **Caffè Florian** has paid host to the passing of history: Casanova and Goldoni were among its patrons and then, later, Lord Byron, Goethe and Rousseau. Brought into existence by Floriano Francesconi, from whom it derives its name, it preserves in tact an unblemished charm all of its own. **Caffè Quadri**, founded just a little later (1775) has also opened its doors to an array of famous personalities including Ruskin, Dumas and Proust. During the Austrian occupation of Venice, it was the favorite haunt of the military and became known as Kaffehaus. Its elegant and splendidly frescoed rooms are seeped in the compelling charm of bygone eras.

Harry's Bar, in Calle Vallaresso, was opened in 1931 by Giuseppe Cipriani thanks to the generous financial help of an American from Boston called Harry.

Among its most famous patrons was Ernest Hemingway who became a regular. Even to the present day it has remained a favorite haunt of Americans who want to sample the celebrated "Bellini" cocktail, a delicious aperitif made with white wine and peach juice, invented by Cipriani himself.

There are two different ways of making coffee.

The first is to pour coarsely ground coffee over boiling water to produce an infusion. A variant of this method is Turkish coffee.

The second is the Italian method of percolating finely ground coffee through a stream of boiling hot water. The coffee can be made in a Neapoli-

Goldoni made a comedy of it

Around 1750, the great writer Goldoni wrote a comedy around the compelling character of Don Marzio entitled, La Bottega del Caffè *(the Coffeeshop) which mirrored the customs and chit-chat of the noble Venetians which found daily expression in the cafes as opposed to the taverns used by the poorer classes.*

IN PADUA

The famous **Caffè Pedrocchi** was founded in 1831 by Antonio Pedrocchi and designed by

the architect Giuseppe Jappelli. During the 19th century it was the favorite haunt of artists and patriots and is still a meeting place for Padua's university students. Its many rooms are extremely elegant and its façade is a sight to see.

IN VERONA

Here the most famous café is the **Antico Caffè Dante** which was founded in 1870 during the Austrian domination of Verona and which still preserves all the charm of the period when Verona was a prestigious city. Embellished with a garden seating more than 150 people, this delightful café boasts a fish-based restaurant as well as all the traditional pastries and desserts.

This is by no means a comprehensive guide to Veneto's historical cafés of which there are many among which it's worth noting the **Caffè Franchin** in Rovigo and the **Caffè Biffi** in Treviso.

Above left: *the* Caffè Florian*; above: gentlemen in a café, from a 17th century Venetian print; the* Caffè Pedrocchi *in Padua.*
The photos of coffee-pots and cups are taken from Dal Caffè all'Espresso, by Francesco and Riccardo Illy, the celebrated coffee-producers.

Tea or coffee? Two different worlds

Once upon a time, everyone's favorite drink was chocolate. Today, the most popular drinks are tea and coffee. The Earth's population is divided up into two groups: the coffee drinkers and the tea drinkers. Coffee, which originated in the East, has become the most popular drink in the West. Since the 18th century, it has become a symbol of intellectual lucidity, slightly exotic and even, perhaps, erotic – its strong flavor and black color perhaps calling to mind the underworld. It did not become popular immediately. The renowned physician-poet Francesco Redi was a staunch critic of coffee for many years at the 17th century court of Grandduke Cosimo de' Medici – until he too was converted to the "Islamic brew".

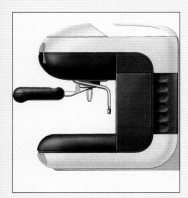

tan coffee-pot, a moka coffee-pot, or an espresso machine.
A striking espresso machine designed by Giugiaro appears in the photo on the left.

Since espresso is an emulsion and a suspension at the same time, it has aroma and texture as well as taste. Espresso should be served in a warm cup thick enough to absorb part of the coffee's heat.

The spell of a unique city

VENICE

Piazza San Marco

An aerial view of Piazza San Marco. Left: the winged lion, symbol of the Republic.

Stunningly beautiful, **Piazza San Marco** has amassed a unique wealth of symbols to the grandeur and power Venice once enjoyed in the world. The focal point of the square and its religious symbol is the large exotic **Basilica**; **Palazzo Ducale** is a testament to the city's political power during its golden period; the treasury and legal procedures of the old Republic are symbolized by the former offices of the Procurators known as the **Procuratie**; while Venice's great cultural heritage is represented by the **Libreria Marciana**.

No less than fourteen lions, symbol of the Republic, stand on guard and look out to sea, the source of the city's wealth and spirit.

Any visitor to Venice ought to try and conjure up, through a leap of imagination, the great events which have taken place in the city through the centuries, the parades, the processions, festivals and ceremonies, not forgetting the still existing *carnival*, which was and still is one of the most famous in the world. The attention of the visitor is immediately attracted by the impressive splendor of the Basilica, but it's worth noting that a thousand years ago, the Batario canal divided the square in half which then had two churches and a

ing the 14th and 15th centuries acquired its Gothic character, while **Palazzo Ducale** owes its elegant Moorish harmony to the fact that it was an old castle.
The **Torre dell'Orologio** was built at the beginning of the 1500s and is the work of the brothers **Paolo** and **Carlo Ranieri**. It was in-

Take away from Venice

First and foremost, what one takes away from Venice is the memory of its golden spires and bewitching waterways. But for anyone wanting to take home a more tangible souvenir Venice boasts a long tradition in the manufacturing of various fine objects. For example, Venice boasts a splendid line in embroidery and fine silk fabrics (the former based in **Burano**, the latter in **Asolo**). **Glass** is another thriving industry in Venice and you'll find all manner of glass objects in the city's shops including lampshades, sculptures and small glass animals. There are also the famous Venetian mirrors, dolls, everything relating to bookbinding as well as masks, ceramics and carnival costumes.

hospital. The canal was then covered and the **Procuratie Vecchie** built though originally it had only one floor. What today is the *Campanile* was once a tower overlooking the sea. Only in the 18th century did the piazza acquire the aspect it has today.
In the meantime the Basilica, which is almost a thousand years old, had been built and, dur-

valuable to sailors as it showed not only the time but the phases of the moon enabling them to work out the tides. The 16th century was the golden formative period of the piazza: the Procuratie Vecchie, destroyed by a fire, was rebuilt in the form we see today and the architect **Sansovino** designed the Libreria Marciana. At the end of the 1500s, the

Above: *the* Procuratie Vecchie *and, in the background, the Ala Napoleonica, home of the* Museo Correr. Left: *the elegant* Loggetta *by* Sansovino.

The time between east and west

The **Torre del-l'Orologio**, located to the north of Piazza San Marco was designed in the 1400s by **Mauro Codussi**. This splendid astronomical clock depicts the phases of the moon and the zodiac in blue and gold enamel. It would appear that the clock was used by sailors when they wanted to embark as they could read from it the times of high and low tides. The two bronze Moors which strike the hour with an impressive mechanical movement are of the same period.

Procuratie Nuove was erected, begun by **Scamozzi** and completed by **Longhena**.

At the beginning of the 19th century Napoleon had the **Ala Napoleonica** built which completes the piazza and is the home of the **Correr Museum**.

In 1902, the *Campanile* suddenly collapsed but was immediately rebuilt and a magnificent panoramic view of the city can be enjoyed from its summit.

The **Libreria Marciana** also deserves a special mention, both as a building in itself and for the treasures it contains. Boasting over a million volumes, it is one of Italy's most

important libraries. Among all the masterpieces on its shelves, besides the many nautical maps which narrate the centuries-old maritime adventures of the Serene Republic, one deserves a special mention: the *Breviario Grimani* (Grimani was a 16th century cardinal), a Flemish masterpiece in the 14 and 1500s. An interesting fact is that the early nucleus of the library was founded thanks to a donation of books by the poet Petrarch from his own library, to which was added, in the 1400s, the large collection of volumes owned by the great Humanist, Cardinal Bessarione.

The building it-

Walking through Venice
The sestieri, sottoporteghi and campielli

In Venice it is worth noting that the roads are called calle *or* campielli*. The canals obviously are of the utmost importance and known locally as* rii*. The covered walkways go by the name of* sottoporteghi *while the small public recreation areas are known as* corti*.*

Venice is divided up into six districts or sestieri *and the city's buildings are numbered according to which sestiere they belong.*

self, combining a very distinctive Venetian style with classical undertones, is attributed to **Sansovino** and was built in the middle of the 1500s. It is graced by a series of Gothic arches, Ionic columns and a rooftop terrace. The interior boasts works by some of histo-

On the facing page, left: *the* Orologio della Torre; *the* moors *that strike the hour; the* Torre dell'Orologio; *a drawing of the section of the* Campanile; *the* Campanile.
This page: *the* Libreria Marciana *by* Sansovino.
Right: "Venice Carnival" (photo Fulvio Roiter).
Below: one of the most famous cafés in Piazza San Marco.

ry's finest artists. Several works by **Veronese** adorn the ceiling of the *Salone* together with a fresco of *Wisdom* by **Titian**. Next door to the Libreria Marciana is the old **Palazzo Zecca**, this too designed by **Sansovino**. This was the mint which produced all those chunky coins – gold shields and silver ducats – that represented Venice's huge power and influence in the world.

Let's now return to the piazza which, though vast, enjoys the intimate embrace of the spectacular array of buildings that enclose it. Together with the golden lions, the three **Pili** rise in front of the doors of the Basilica which were, in point of fact, ship masts built in the 15th century. On public holidays the red and gold standards of the Republic are unfurled and left to flutter in the wind.

At the far end of the area between the Basilica and the waterfront known as the **Piazzetta**, stand two red and grey granite columns, originating from the East, which are topped by statues of Venice's patron saints: St Theodore, the old protector of the Republic, and St Mark in the guise of a winged lion. As Venice has done for centuries, they both overlook the sea. A more circumstantial and relaxed way of observing what the square has to offer and where you can let your mind wander to the accompaniment of a small orchestra can be had by sitting in one of two historic cafés in the square: *Caffè Florian* and *Caffè Quadri*.

Special events in Venice

The city's festival season is opened by the **Venice Carnival** that every February offers a grand spectacle of color and revelry which attracts people from all over the world and lasts for days on end.

On April 25, Venice celebrates the **Festa di San Marco** in honor of its patron saint. This involves gondola races and free roses handed out to lovers. On the second Sunday of May, the **Regata della Sensa** takes place during which the historical and famous marriage between the Doge and the sea (see the spotlight on "La Serenissima"). Perhaps the most eagerly awaited event in Venice is the **Festa del Redentore** which takes place on the third Saturday of July and consists of ceremonial boat processions and fireworks. On the first Sunday of September, the gondola race known as the **Regata Storica** is held on the Grand Canal.

At the end of March, there's the **International Film Festival** and from June through to September, the **Biennale d'Arte**.

The Basilica of San Marco

The sumptuous blend of styles and especially the strong eastern influences which have gone into the creation of the **Basilica of San Marco** make it a unique religious building not only in Italy but in the whole of Christendom. Through the centuries, Venice always had a strong trading rapport with the East and eastern influences abound where the Basilica is concerned, made manifest in the multiple cupolas, the spires and the ornamental decoration.

The Basilica is almost a thousand years old. Previously, a temple had stood on the site which the Venetians erected to enshrine the remains of St Mark that they had captured from the Mohammedans in 828. St Mark then replaced St Theodore as the city's patron saint who had too many associations with the Byzantine world. However, it was only in 1807 that the Basilica became Venice's cathedral.

Ever since its creation, the Basilica has had a part to play in the history of Venice. It was from here that the Fourth Crusade set sail and here that the reconciliation took place between the the throne of Peter and Barbarossa and Pope Alexander III. From here too the war ships set sail against the Genoa Republic.

Enriched through the centuries, the Basilica is laid out in the form of a Greek cross and has five domes, though no one knows who designed them. Two orders of five arches adorn the façade which, at ground level, have five doorways decorated with bas-reliefs depicting the *Sacred History*, the *Arts* and the *Crafts*. A large stained-glass window which illuminates the interior graces the upper central series of arches. The *Tribuna* contains the famous bronze *Quattro Cavalli* whose origin, whether Greek or Roman, remains uncertain (some attribute them to **Lisippo**) which arrived in Venice at the beginning of the 13th century as war booty and since then have come to represent Venetian liberty. Napoleon carried off the four bronze horses to France but they were returned to Venice in 1815. The horses you'll see today on the façade are a copy of the originals.

On the right-hand side of the Basilica stand two square columns which arrived in Venice in 1256. On the corner of the Basilica can be found the *Gruppo dei Tetrarchi*, thought to be Syrian works. These are porphyry sculptures believed to represent the Roman emperors, Diocletian, Maximillian, Valerius and Constantine.

Left: the interior of San Marco; Madonna Nicopeia, a Byzantine panel from the 10th century. Below: the women's gallery of the Basilica.

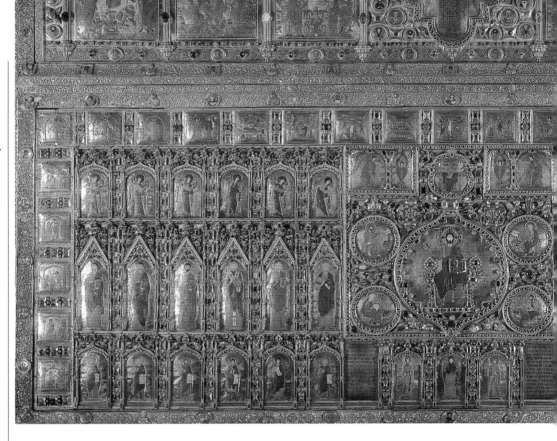

The treasury of San Marco

The **Pala d'Oro** is a stunning gold altarpiece comprising of almost three thousand precious stones and eighty enamels, most of which probably came from Constantinople. The work as a whole, set within a Gothic frame, bears the signature of **Gian Paolo Boninsegna**. Steadily enriched through the centuries, it finally acquired the form it has today in the era of **Duke Andrea Dandolo**. The Pala is the most valuable object in the **Treasury of San Marco** where you can also see a collection of *icons*, *sacred vestments*, *chalices* and other liturgical objects, all contained within one of the towers of the old **Palazzo Ducale** and many of which were brought back from Constantinople to enrich Venice's cultural heritage.

The interior of the Basilica is simply dazzling as a result of the mosaics, the golds and silvers and the stunning choreography of the colonnades.

The floor of the Basilica is entirely covered in marble and follows a distinctly dual decorative design thanks to the use, on the one hand, of regular mosaic tiles and, on the other, an assemblage of different irregular stones.

Lifting one's gaze to head height, one encounters the sacred area separated from the congregation, the *Iconostasi*, where the **High Altar** can be found, secluded by an arcade of columns linked by a balustrade and overlooked by a collection of statues of *Apostles and Saints* grouped around a *Crucifix* by **Dalle Masegne**. The overall effect is resplendent of 14th century Gothic design.

Here, below the high altar, stands the *urn* which contains the remains of St Mark and also the famous **Pala d'Oro** (see facing column). But it is the dazzling gold of the mosaics that pervade the entire Basilica which constitutes the real charm of this building. The workmanship was probably carried out by a collective of unknown Byzantine craftsmen; it wasn't until the 15th and 16th centuries that illustrious artists began enriching the Basilica with their works. The expressive culmination of the Byzantine influence is probably best represented by the ***Arcone della Passione*** with the depictions of the *Life of Jesus*; counteracting this is the splendor of the mosaic of the ***Atrio nella cupola*** dedicated to *Genesis* which depicts the *Creation of the World*.

If these are the aesthetic wonders, the sacred center of the Basilica is represented by the most venerated image inside San Marco, the *Vergine Nicopeia* ("Bringer of Victory") which was stolen from Constantinople and became a symbol of maritime Venice. It's a Byzantine painting from around the 10th century which sits inside a magnificent gilt frame inlaid with precious stones and is kept in the *Chapel* to which it gives its name.

The **Baptistery** contains a *baptismal font*, the building of which several artists had a hand in: **Tiziano Minio**, **Desiderio da Firenze** and

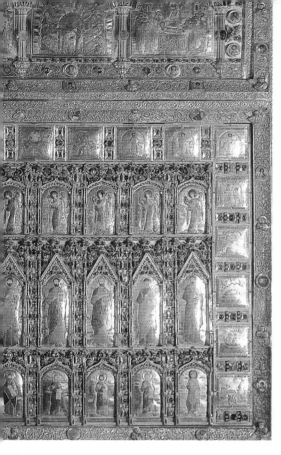

Francesco Segala to a design by **Sansovino**. Segala was also responsible for the statue of *St John the Baptist*.

The Baptistery contains many tombs of doges as well as the *tomb of* the Veneto artist *Sansovino*. Legend has it that Christ rested on the granite slab of the altar while preaching to his disciples. The mosaics adorning the walls are from the 14th century and depict the *Life of John the Baptist* and *Jesus*.

From the Baptistery, one enters the *Cappella Zen*, the burial chapel of Cardinal Giovan Battista Zen, on whose altar is the famous bronze statue of the *Madonna*, a gift of the lower class population to the Holy Virgin. The tomb of the cardinal stands at the center.

Above: *the famous* **Horses** *on the façade of the* **Basilica of San Marco.**

Below left: *the interior of the* **Baptistery** *and the* **Gruppo dei Tetrarchi.**

Palazzo Ducale

The construction of the **Palazzo Ducale** took two long centuries. This splendid vast building rises near Piazza San Marco on the site of the preceding towered castle. Many hands went into its design and construction – **Dalle Masegne, Pietro Lombardo**, **Antonio Rizzi** and **Pietro Lamberti**. One of its singular characteristics that goes against all architectural rules but endows it with an elegance of its own, is to present its empty spaces below and its solid unbroken walls higher up. At ground level, there's a long *portico* with, above, a *loggia* adorned with balconies and the upper storey is decorated with colorful geometric arabesques. The roof is crenelated in a Byzantine style. The splendid high Gothic *Porta della Carta* (1438), superintended by a winged lion and a statue of the doge, *Francesco Foscari*, leads into the stately *cortile* where, to the north, stand the *Porticato* and the *Arco Foscari* in front of the *Scala dei Giganti*, a monumental staircase with statues of *Neptune* and *Mars* by **Sansovino** and, higher above, the façade of the *Orologio*.

A visit to the Palazzo Ducale is rich in surprises and stimulating encounters. The *Scala dei Censori* leads to the *Piano delle Logge* and here is where can be found the **Loggia Foscari**. The *Scala d'Oro* (the golden stairway), created by **Sansovino** and **Scarpagnino**, leads to the higher floors which include the **Casa del Doge** (the residence of the Duke) where the marbles and stuccos are by **Alessandro Vittoria**. The palace was once a veritable powerhouse, being

both the residence of the duke and his court and the seat of the highest magistrature of the Venetian Republic. In the old residence of the duke there's a splendid *Leone di San Marco* painted by **Carpaccio** as well as important pictures by **Bellini** and **Bosch**.

There now begins the long tour of the salons, beginning with the *Salone del Maggior Consiglio* (the Great Council Chamber): this is where the Venetian nobility – there is space for a thousand people – elected the doge. A large *Paradise* by **Tintoretto** hangs above the *Tribuna*. Other works to be found here include paintings by **Palma il Giovane** and **Bassano** as well as **Veronese**'s stupendous *Apotheosis of Venice*. Portraits of all Venice's doges adorn the *Sala dello Scrutinio* (where the result of the voting was announced) together with a *Last Judgement* by **Palma il Giovane**. A work by **Titian** depicting *Doge Antonio Grimani Kneeling before Faith* can be found in the *Sala delle Quattro Porte* which also contains a fresco by **Tintoretto** celebrating the founding of Venice.

The *Sala del Collegio* is where ambassadors were received in days of old and is followed by the *Sala del Senato* which contains works by **Tintoretto** and **Palma il Giovane**. The *Sala del Consiglio dei Dieci* also contains some

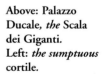

Above: **Palazzo Ducale,** *the* **Scala dei Giganti.**
Left: *the sumptuous* **cortile.**

Above, from left to right: *the famous* Scala d'Oro *and the stately* Sala del Maggior Consiglio.
Right: *the bust of* Doge Venier *by* A. Vittoria.
Below: *two works by* Tintoretto *in the* Sala dell'Anticollegio.

Above: *the* Sala del Maggior Consiglio.
Right: *the* Sala del Consiglio dei Dieci.
Below, left: *the* Sala degli Scarlatti.
Right: *the* Doge Pasquale Cicogna, assisted by St Mark, supplicates Christ, *a work by* Palma il Giovane *in the* Sala del Senato.

fine paintings, including works by **Veronese** and was where the feared **Tribunale dei Delitti Politici** sat when coming to a verdict regarding all crimes against the State. A double revolving door gives its name to the *Sala della Bussola* that contains the box known as the "bocche di leone" (the lion's mouth) where anyone could insert a note denouncing anonymously someone they believed guilty of a crime.

There is then the *Sala degli Inquisitori di Stato*, office of the State inquisitors and the *Armory* which contains a wide collection of weapons used during the Venetian Republic's various wars. A *Bust of Francesco Morosini* in bronze overlooks the array of swords, halberds, hackbuts, pikes and culverins.

Rather less glamorous are the twenty or so *Celle dei Pozzi* (the prison cells) with their bare stone walls. More cells, known as the *Piombi* are to be found in the vicinity of the roof of the palazzo where the prisoners were subjected to extreme heat in the summer and extreme cold in the winter.

Finally, there's the famous **Ponte dei Sospiri** (the Bridge of Sighs) which unites the *Sala del Tribunale* (the law court) to the **Prigioni Nuove** (the New Prison) built at the beginning of the 18th century when the prisons inside the palazzo were no longer considered suitable.

From Rialto to Sospiri

The bridges of Venice

Of all Venice's bridges, the **Ponte di Rialto** is not only the most famous but also the oldest of the three which span the Grand Canal. Originally made of wood, it collapsed in the 1400s and was rebuilt with an ingenious mechanism which allowed the the taller river craft to pass beneath it. A final reconstruction was carried out in 1592 by the architect **Antonio Da Ponte** whose project triumphed over rival designs by Palladio and Sansovino. Possessing only one arch, 28 meters long, the Rialto is 7.50 meters high at its tallest point. The bridge has three walkways divided by a total of twenty-four shops and offers a splendid panoramic view of the Grand Canal.

Of a completely different nature is the **Ponte**

Above, left: *the* Ponte di Rialto *and the same bridge between the gondolas of the Grand Canal.* **Below:** *the* Ponte degli Scalzi.

The Bridge of Sighs between Palazzo Ducale and the Prison.

dei Sospiri (the Bridge of Sighs) which joins the **Palazzo Ducale** to the **Prigioni Nuove**. It was built in the 1600s, the Baroque era, by **Antonio Contin**. Its name derives from the fact that prisoners were escorted across it to the prison and caught what was often their last glimpse of Venice from its windows.

Less important but no less elegant and harmonious is the **Ponte degli Scalzi**, also known as **Ponte della Stazione** as it's the first bridge one encounters on the Grand Canal heading towards San Marco. Though it takes up the Venetian style, it was built only recently, in 1934, in white Istrian stone. It was designed by **Eugenio Miozzi** to replace the 19th century metal bridge which had previously occupied the site. It's 40 meters long and 7 meters high at the center.

Venice is of course graced with countless bridges, many of which, though overshadowed by the three famous ones, are delightful and offer bewitching views of the city.

The lagoon in Piazza San Marco
When high tides invade Venice

A curious and periodic occurrence in Venice is the phenomenon of the high tides, known locally as "acqua alta" when the waters invade Piazza San Marco and the Basilica, sometimes reaching levels of half a meter.

The Venetians however have gotten used to this picturesque inconvenience and will resort to tiny boats in order to carry on with their daily business; at times even the occasional gondola will appear in the famous Piazza.

The phenomenon of the high tides relates to a complicated problem – the safety and survival of a city that is under constant siege from the tides – a problem which, despite various studies, has still not been completely solved. The problem of controlling the water levels of Venice's canals has, in fact, become one of the toughest challenges facing international hydraulic engineering.

Santa Maria della Salute, the Baroque basilica reflected on the Grand Canal

Built in response to the Venetians demand to commemorate the end of a plague, the church contains masterpieces by Tintoretto and Titian

The **Basilica of Santa Maria della Salute** stands near the Punta della Dogana where it throws its reflection onto the waters of the Grand Canal. It was begun in 1631 by the young Baldassarre Longhena as a commission for the Senate who intended it as a tribute to

The octagonal interior, with the elegant pavement, of Santa Maria della Salute. Above: *a view of the* Basilica.

the Madonna for having ended a terrible plague. Its construction was completed in 1687.

The church is the fruit of an ingenious architectural invention, and takes the form of an octagon with a large *cupola* and a smaller dome over the *sanctuary*. It was designed in the shape of a crown, a possible reference to the Queen of Heaven who was supplicated in times of plague; a statue of the *Virgin* stands atop the cupola.

This church has always been venerated by the Venetians but this is especially the case every November 21 when a procession takes place which involves the entire city and a makeshift bridge is constructed for the occasion to unite

Above: *the impressive white façade of* Santa Maria della Salute.
Above, right: *the elegant* Punta della Dogana *next to the church.*
Right: *the interior of the* cupola *of* Santa Maria della Salute.

the Basilica with the opposite bank of the canal. The stately interior is octagonal in form with arcades on which sits the drum of the cupola and has six lateral *chapels*. It also contains some fine works of art. A marble group of sculptures by **Josse Le Court** depicts the plague fleeing before the Madonna, in memory of the Basilica's origins. Fine works by **Titian** include his *Pentecost* (third altar on the left) and, in the *sacristy*, the *Death of Abel*, the *Sacrifice of Abraham*, *David and Goliath*; there's also a young work of his of *St Mark and Saints* painted in 1512. Finally, there's the *Marriage at Cana* by **Tintoretto**.

Santa Maria Gloriosa dei Frari, home of Titian's Assumption

Above: *three aisles and twelve columns grace the interior of* Santa Maria Gloriosa dei Frari. Left: *the façade of the church.*

Below: Giovanni Bellini*'s altarpiece of the* Enthroned Madonna with Saints.

This enormous church that stands in the square which bears its name, is one of the most important in Venice, an honor it enjoys partly because of the number of splendid artistic masterpieces contained within its walls. Begun by the Franciscans in 1340, the Frari was not finished until more than a century later. The brick façade with its central *rose window* is not particularly distinguished. The interior however is of great interest, beginning with the magnificent *choir* which contains no less than 124 stalls. The church also contains many *tombs*, including that of *Antonio Canova* which he designed himself. There are also

the tombs of various doges, including *Doge Niccolò Tron*, a 15th century work, and the 17th century monument to *Doge Giovanni Pesaro*, executed by **Longhena**. In the vastness of the Basilica be careful not to miss **Donatello**'s wooden sculpture of *St John the Baptist* which can be found in the first apsidal chapel on the right. There's an admirable triptych of the *Madonna and Saints and An-*

Titian: the **Assumption of the Virgin,** *one of the most famous paintings of 16th century art.*

gels by **Giovanni Bellini** on the altar of the *sacristy*. However, the two real masterpieces of the Frari are both the work of the great **Titian**: the *Assumption of the Virgin* and the *Pesaro Altarpiece*.

As can be seen the Frari contains works of art belonging to various periods and styles which span a huge stretch of time and reach an artistic peak with the works of Bellini and Titian.

Below: the equestrian statue of Bartolomeo Colleoni by Andrea Verrocchio.

Below, right: the church of San Giovanni e Paolo.

Church of San Giovanni e Paolo
Home of artistic masterpieces and watched by the equestrian statue of Colleoni

The Dominican **church of San Giovanni and Paolo** (which the Venetians, joining the two names, call **San Zanipolo**) stands in the *campo* of the same name. It has a brick façade and five elegant apsidal *chapels*. It was begun at the beginning of the 1300s and its construc-

tion was to continue for almost a century. Like the Frari, it contains many *tombs*, including those of the *Doge Giovanni Mocenigo* (1485) by **Pietro Lombardo**, *Doge Andrea Vendramin*, also attributed to Lombardo and *Doge Marco Cornèr*, to the left of the high altar, which is adorned with beautiful statues by **Nino Pisano**. Other tombs are dedicated to *Tomaso Mocenigo* (Gothic), *Niccolò Marcello* and *Pasquale Malipiero* (the latter two being the work of Pietro Lombardo).

The church also contains some fine paintings like **Piazzetta**'s *Glory*, ceiling paintings by **Paolo Veronese**, a 14th century depiction of *Christ carrying the Cross* by **Alvise Vivarini** and **Giovanni Bellini**'s *triptych of St Vincent Ferrer*.

Right: *the interior of the* church of San Giovanni e Paolo. Below: *the asymmetrical façade of the* Scuola Grande di San Marco.

The Scuola Grande di San Marco

To the left of the church of Giovanni and Paolo on the picturesque Rio dei Mendicanti is this school, one of what were the six principle schools in Venice and, in common with the others, owed its origins to the religious orders (in particular, the Dominicans and Franciscans).

It is now the city hospital which occupies the entire convent, including five *cloisters*.
The **Scuola Grande di San Marco** was built on a design by **Pietro Lombardo** and was completed by **Mauro Codussi**. Later, **Sansovino** had a hand in enlarging it.

The asymmetrical façade is beautiful and quintessentially Venetian Renaissance in style with its trompe-l'oeil reliefs and colored marble. A *statue of St Mark* and another of *Charity* adorn the façade.

Other Churches in Venice

Built in different eras and different styles, Venice is graced by many churches, many of which contain great works of art. Here are a but a few

In the Castello quarter Santa Maria Formosa

Situated in the Sestiere of Castello, the **church of Santa Maria Formosa** dates back to the 12th century and was rebuilt by **Mauro Coducci** in 1492. It is distinguished by two classical façades and a Baroque **campanile**. The interior contains a triptych by **Bartolomeo Vivarini** depicting the Nativity, a Madonna of Mercy and the Meeting of Joachim and St Anna.

San Rocco and the Scuola Grande di San Rocco, a monument to the art of Tintoretto

Patron of the sick, St Roch's remains are preserved in this church which bears his name. It was begun at the beginning of the 15th century and finished two centuries later. The façade is the work of **Maccaruzzi** who also designed the nearby **Scuola di San Rocco**. Various statues by **Marchiori** adorn the façade including one of St Roch being carried to Heaven by Angels. The façade however is dominated by a panel depicting St Roch Ministering to the Plague-Stricken.

The 18th century Chiesa di San Barnaba in Dorsoduro

In the square bearing its name stands the **church of San Barnaba** which was built in the middle of the 1700s by **Lorenzo Boschetti** and is enriched by the addition of a 14th century **campanile**. The interior vault is adorned with frescoes by **Cedini**, a follower of **Tiepolo**, depicting **St Barnabas in Glory**. There's also a beautiful Holy Family by **Paolo Veronese**.

San Moisé on the picturesque street of the same name

In the San Marco district stands the **church of San Moisé** *which was built in the 8th century and then rebuilt two centuries later by* **Moisé Venier**. *The church contains some fine works of art: a marble* Pietà *by* **Corradini**, *a* Making of the Cross *by* **Liberi** *and a* Deposition *by* **Roccatagliata**. *The Baroque* **high altar** *is especially impressive. The church contains two other superb paintings – a* Last Supper *by* **Palma il Giovane** *and a* Washing of the Feet *by* **Tintoretto**.

The beautiful 15th century San Zaccaria

Dating back to the 10th century, this beautiful church was rebuilt in the middle of the 1400s with a multi-levelled façade, a masterpiece of Venetian Renaissance design. This church too contains some fine works of art including **Giovanni Bellini**'s Madonna and Saints *and three carved gilt* polyptychs *by* **Vivarini**. *There are paintings by* **Tiepolo** *and* **Tintoretto** *in the* chapel of Sant'Atanasio.

The island of San Giorgio Maggiore with Palladio's impressive basilica

On the island of San Giorgio rises the white basilica built between 1565 and 1580 by *Andrea Palladio* and finished half a century later by *Scamozzi*. The façade is the fruit of intensive mathematical studies of proportion by Palladio and is designed to create a harmony with the church's aisled interior. Two *statues of St George* and *St Stephen* adorn the façade as well as *busts of the doges Memmo* and *Ziani*. The *campanile* is the 18th century work of *Benedetto Buratti*.

The Fondazione Cini, a prestigious cultural center, is based on the island of San Giorgio.

Spotlight on *THE SERENISSIMA*

Venice, the Doge, the sea

*Eight centuries of great naval feats;
a stable government led by one man, the duke,
assisted by a council: many victories in war.
Trade routes and markets conquered in the Orient.
A long and lavish reign of prosperity highlighted by
cultural and artistic splendors*

A history on the seas

In the 9th century the traders of Rivoalto were already in Alexandria and brought from there the treasures of Saint Mark's which were to form the wealth, not only in symbolical and religious terms, of the future republic.

Since then, first on the side of Byzantium, then against the Byzantine forces, Venice became not only the ruler of the Adriatic but also the chief naval power of the time, a power which reached its peak in the 15th century. Venetian galleys had to fend off many attacks along the Mediterranean from hostile invaders eager to get their hands on the huge bounty of riches possessed by the Republic. The victory against the Turks at Lepanto in 1571, heralded as a historic triumph, marked in reality the decline of Venice as a world power. Trade routes between the West and the Orient were now beginning to be ruled by other powers. The irrevocable dwindling of Venetian power was to arrive later with the loss of the Peloponnese to the Turks, the eternal enemy of the *Serenissima*, in 1714. The final fatal blow to the Venetian Republic arrived in 1797 when Napoleon occupied Venice and destroyed the city's arsenal and all its ships.

The Duke and his powers

For almost a thousand years, the Republic of Venice was controlled by one figure whose power was of a democratic-tyranical nature. In fact, the political and military powers possessed by the Duke were enormous as were the honors granted him.
The Doge would be elected for life, but by way of a complex electoral system which precluded preventive agreements. The Doge was assisted by the Lower Council, while legislative power was entrusted to the Higher Council (400 members). Executive power was in the hands of the Senate; while judiciary and police powers were handled by the Council of Ten.

Celebrities of Venetian history

*The Duke
Francesco Morosini*

*The Duke
Leonardo Loredan*

*The Duke
Vincenzo Querini*

In order to know more. Two rich and fascinating museums document the maritime history of Venice – the *Museo Correr* in St Mark's Square and the *Museo Storico Navale*, near the Arsenale. The Correr Museum contains the perspective map of *Jacopo de' Barbari*, an entire room dedicated to the *Bucintoro* – the the doges' ceremonial barge, another given over to the arsenale and the dockyard workers. There are also models of ships and galleys as well as a 17th-century gun ship complete with twelve canon holes. The three-storeyed Museo Storico Navale traces the history of the Venetian navy through the centuries. It contains many models of various kinds of ships, artillery pieces, navigational instruments, heirlooms from the dukes and a magnificent model of the Bucintoro.

A boat made of gold: the Bucintoro

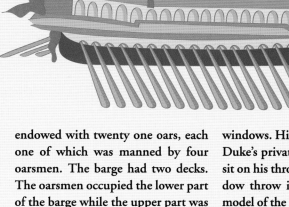

The *Bucintoro* was the large ceremonial barge used by the Duke in the centuries of the Republic. It was a large, lavish craft with carvings, statues, gold embellishments and velvets employed in official ceremonies, on occasion of the investiture of the new duke and especially to celebrate the yearly festival of the "Sposalizio del Mare" on the day of the Ascension. The early Bucintoro did not have oars but were instead pulled along by other boats. Later the Bucintoro was endowed with twenty one oars, each one of which was manned by four oarsmen. The barge had two decks. The oarsmen occupied the lower part of the barge while the upper part was covered by a baldachin and red velvets and boasted ninety seats and forty one windows. Higher still was located the Duke's private room where he would sit on his throne and from a little window throw into the sea the ring. A model of the last Bucintoro, destroyed by the French, can still be seen in the *Museo Storico della Marina*.

The ceremony of the Sposalizio col Mare

(which still takes place every year on the second Sunday of May)

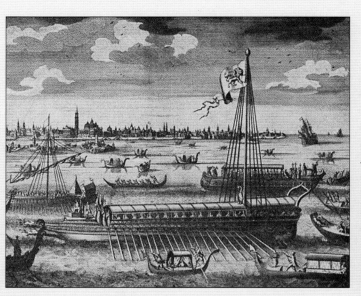

In 1177, a historic reconciliation took place in San Marco in Venice between Federigo Barbarossa and Pope Alexander III and mediated by the Duke Sebastiano Ziani.
This event was to sanction Venice's future dominion over the Adriatic. On that occasion the Pope gave a precious ring to the Duke with an invitation that he marry the sea as a token of his recognized dominion. Ever since then the majestic ceremony known as the Sposalizio col Mare has taken place every year on the day of the Ascension and still continues to this day. The Duke takes his place on the Bucintoro, followed by a procession of ships, boats and gondolas which sail out as far as the stone lighthouse where, turning the stern of the Bucintoro towards the open sea, he throws into the sea the "vera" – the gold ring (a valuable copy of the ring he wears on his hand) and pronounces the words: "Ti sposiamo, o mare, in segno di vero e perpetuo dominio" (We marry you the sea, as a sign of true and perpetual dominion).

The Grand Canal

*On the waterway which both divides and unites
the city stand all the most beautiful Venetian palaces whose
reflected marble façades shimmer in the water*

Weaving its way from **Piazzale Roma** as far as the **San Marco** basin four kilometers of waterway span the entire city of Venice. We are referring, of course, to the splendid **Grand Canal**, one of the most impressive and unique thoroughfares in the world. Not surprisingly, in the course of history, most of Venice's most beautiful palaces have sprung up along the banks of the canal where their reflections shimmer in the water in an otherworldly enchantment of color and exotic design. Add to this bewitching spectacle the occasional large church, the Rialto bridge, the bobbing gondolas and hanging gardens and you're looking at a panorama that will elicit a gasp of wonder from even the most hardened cynic.

Above: *view of the Grand Canal taken from Ponte degli Scalzi.* Below: *Palazzo Loredan and Palazzo Farsetti, Veneto-Byzantine buildings and today the town hall.*

Beginning our journey from the left bank at the **Dogana da Mar** (customs house) and the nearby tower on whose summit there's a golden globe, symbolizing good fortune, we pass the **Chiesa della Salute** and then encounter a series of splendid palaces – **Palazzo Dario**, designed by **Pietro Lombardo**, followed immediately by **Palazzo Venier dei Leoni**, the 18th century palace which is now the home of the **Guggenheim Collection** and the 16th century **Palazzo Contarini Dal Zaffo**.

Having passed the **Galleria dell'Accademia** and **Palazzo Contarini degli Scrigni**, we now see reflected on the waters of the Grand Canal the Gothic 15th century **Palazzo Loredan**, home of the Austrian Embassy in Venice. At this point the tourist might want to stop off at **Ca' Rezzonico**, designed by **Longhena**, and pay a visit to the museum celebrating the life and culture of Venice in the 18th century (see the Museums section in this guide for more information).

Two similar adjoining buildings follow – **Palazzo Giustinian** and **Palazzo Foscari**, this latter now part of the University. Napoleon

resided for a brief spell in **Palazzo Balbi**, distinctive for the obelisks on its roof. This is followed by **Palazzo Pisani-Moretta** and **Palazzo Barbarigo della Terrazzi**, so-called for the terrace and hanging garden with which it is graced.

Thus, on the right bank, we arrive at **Palazzo Grimani** with its 16th century Renaissance façade and broad arches and then the 18th century **Palazzo Corner della Regina**, which was the site of the dwelling of Caterina Cornero, the 15th century queen of Cyprus.

We now arrive at **Ca' Pesaro**, one of the most stately and impressive Venetian palaces. It was designed by **Longhena** and completed at the beginning of the 1700s by **Antonio Gasparri**. It is now the home of the **Galleria d'Arte Moderna**. After the **Chiesa di San Stae** with its Baroque façade, we encounter another of **Longhena**'s creations, **Palazzo Belloni-Battagia** and then the **Fondaco del Megio**, Venice's old granary.

On our right we can now admire the Gothic 15th century **Palazzo Contarini-Fasan**, followed by

Above, left: Ca' Rezzonico, *home of the city's collection of 18th century art;* right: Ca' Foscari, *once the residence of Doge Francesco Foscari and now part of Venice's university.* Above: *gondolas on the Grand Canal.* Left: Palazzo Corner della Regina, *today home of the* Monte di Pietà.

Palazzo Gritti, now owned by one of the most prestigious hotels in Venice. A little further along the canal is **Palazzo Corner della Ca' Grande** and then **Palazzo Giustinian-Lolin**, yet another work by **Longhena** who here merely modified a pre-existing Gothic 14th century building. Still on the right bank, we now encounter the splendid and well-known **Palazzo Grassi** whose façade is broken by a double row of terraces. This is now a venue for important international exhibitions. Our journey along the Grand Canal continues and we come to **Palazzo Contarini delle Figure**, a 16th century building which owes its name to its two caryatids, followed by **Palazzi Mocenigo Vecchio** and **Nuovo**. These two

Left: Palazzo Grassi,
built by Giorgio
Massari *in 1718,*
is now an arts center
hosting important
Venetian
cultural events.

palaces were the residences of famous Ducal Venetian families and it is said that **Giordano Bruno** was a guest here at the end of the 16th century.

Palazzo Garzoni, a fine example of Gothic architecture, is the next most eminent building on our journey and is followed by the Renaissance **Palazzo Corner Spinelli** and **Palazzo Benzon** where both **Lord Byron** and **Canova** stayed. The intriguing **Fondaco dei Tedeschi** now appears whose façade was once adorned with frescoes painted by **Giorgione** which sadly have now disappeared. Equally striking and almost a

Above: *an aerial*
view of part of the
Grand Canal
and Ponte di Rialto.
Left: *the* Fondaco dei
Tedeschi, *erected in*
1505 on the ruins of
another building
destroyed by fire, is
an example of
Renaissance
architecture. It once
had frescoes on its
façade by Giorgione
and Titian *which*
have since been
destroyed.

At the next landing stage we encounter the famous 15th century **Ca' d'Oro**. So lavish was its decorative design that it was given its name (the gold palace) as a tribute to its splendor and indeed it is one of the most beautiful Gothic palaces in Venice.

Our journey along the Grand Canal is about to come to an end. Worth admiring before this happens though are the **Palazzo Gussoni-Grimani** whose exterior was once adorned with frescoes by **Tintoretto**, the Renaissance **Ca' Vendramin-Calergi**, the 18th century **Palazzo Labia**, frescoed by **Giovan Battista Tiepolo** and, finally, **Palazzo Flangini**, a 17th century building designed by **Giuseppe Sardi**.

Above: *the* Ca' d'Oro *(1440), perhaps the most famous of the palaces on the Grand Canal. Its name derives from the fact that its façade was once gold.*
Center, left: *an image of the* Regata Storica *which once a year animates the Grand Canal with its 18th century choreography.*
Right: Palazzo Ventramin-Calergi, *one of the most elegant buildings of the Renaissance, completed by* Lombardo *in 1509.* Richard Wagner *died here in 1883.*

thousand years old is the **Ca' da Mosto**, a surviving example of an old home doubling up as a warehouse.

For centuries a feature of the canals

The gondola

Composed of 280 pieces of wood, once-upon-a-time sumptuously ornate, today rigorously black, it's one of the most distinctive boats in the world

Uniquely Venetian, the gondola has an asymmetrical form and is a little more than eleven meters long and a meter and a half wide. Its construction is quite complex, since it consists of almost 300 pieces of oak wood including the "forcola" - the poppet for the oars - for which walnut wood is used. In the 18th century more than 1500 gondolas navigated the canals, most of which were more lavishly decorated than today's variety, so much so that a law was passed decreeing that they should be black and unadorned – as they have remained until the present day.

Today, there are around 400 gondoliers, who form a company, and pass down the trade from father to son. They are distinguished by their attire – the blue and white striped shirt, the black suits and the straw hat. The gondola is only very rarely used for fishing and has on its prow an ornament known as "ferro" with six teeth (the six districts of the city). Today, the gondolas are built in small workshops known as "squeri". The rowing method employed by the gondoliers is an art in itself and very distinctive; the gondola moves forward in a rhythm known locally as the "voga veneziana" (the Venetian stroke). The gondola of course exerts its charm over every visitor to Venice and a slow ride in one of these boats along the city's canals to the lilting melody of the gondolier's songs is an essential part of the Venetian experience.

When the city puts back on its crown

Carnevale: the party, the masks, Venice

Wild, sumptuous and upbeat, the Venice carnival signifies the apotheosis of this enchanting and enchanted city

The **Venice carnival** has a very long history and tradition. It began in the 12th century but it wasn't until the 1800s, the epoch of libertines, grand dames and dandies, that it reached its height in terms of splendor and gaiety.

It began immediately after Christmas and came to an end when the bells of San Francesco della Vigna announced the advent of Lent.

It was a great festival of parades, carriages, dancing, masks, games and costumes when all social differences disappeared and the wearing of a mask guaranteed the anonymity of everyone.

A characteristic costume of the carnival was the "bauta", a black hooded cape and the "tabarro", an elegant cloak with which a white mask was usually worn.

The carnival declined in stature during the modern era and was only revived as a public festival in 1980, since when it has again enjoyed the reputation of being one of the world's finest carnivals.

When the lagoon lights up
The regata storica, a recollection of the Republic

On the first Sunday of September Venice remembers and repeats the historic "Sposalizio del Mare"

Many regattas take place in Venice during the year, but the most famous is the **Regata Storica** which takes place on the first Sunday of September. There's a large gondola race in which two gondoliers in each boat row their boats from San Marco, along the Grand Canal as far as Piazzale Roma and then back again to the finish line at the quay at Rio Nuovo. Before the gondola race the impressive regata storica takes place on the Grand Canal.

Ornate boats known as *bissone* fill the Grand Canal, manned by several oarsmen dressed in 18th century costume. The bissone are decorated with embroidery, gold insignia, sea-horses and sirens so as to recall the legendary wealth of the old Republic.

Other regattas and historical festivals in Venice include, on the day of the Assumption of the Virgin, the **Sensa** when the doge on board his Bucintoro celebrated the ritual of marrying Venice with the sea, a tradition which dates back to the 11th century and still continues to this day.

Veneto cuisine: recipes

First courses

PASTA AND WHITE BEANS WITH HAM OFF THE BONE (PASTA E FASOI COL PISTELLO DE PARSUTO). *In a saucepan of cold water add the white beans, pig skin cut into small pieces, the ham bone, the carrots, celery, salt and a few table spoons of olive oil. Leave to boil for two and a half hours. Then, taking out the ham bone, add the tagliatelle pasta with a little pepper and olive oil. Serve luke warm with grated parmesan cheese.*

INGREDIENTS (SERVES FOUR). 200 grams of white beans; 100 grams of pig skin; bone of ham; 200 grams of tagliatelle pasta; 1 onion; carrots; celery; olive oil, salt; pepper and parmesan cheese.

CHICKEN SOUP (ZUPPA DI POLLO). *Sauté a little butter in olive oil with a minced onion, some ham cut up into small pieces and a kilo of chicken also cut up into strips. Cook over a low flame and add three fingers of white wine. When the chicken is cooked serve the soup in bowls with toasted bread cut up into cubes and add grated parmesan cheese.*

INGREDIENTS (SERVES FOUR). 1kg of chicken; olive oil, butter; ham; onion; white wine; parmesan cheese and toasted bread.

GNOCCHI WITH MIXED HERBS (GNOCCHI DE ERBE). *Cut 250 grams of white bread without the crust into cubes and soak in milk. Place in boiling salted water for a few minutes spinach and rosemary or herbs of your choice and then drain them and flavor them in butter, salt, pepper and garlic. Mix the bread, three eggs, the prepared herbs, a handful of flour, butter, salt and pepper. Now form from the mixture form the gnocchi and cook them in boiling salted water for ten minutes. They can be served with a dash of parsley and grated cheese.*

INGREDIENTS (SERVES FOUR). 250 grams of white bread; 200 grams of herbs; 1 glass of milk; 75 grams of flour; 80 grams of butter; 50 grams of grated cheese; parsley; salt; pepper and garlic.

PIGEON BAKED WITH BREAD (SOPA COADA). *Cook the pigeons which should be cut up into quarters in a saucepan. Cook the giblets with a little butter, salt, pepper and tomato sauce. Once cooked, debone the pigeons. Boil the stripped bones in a thick consommé of beef stock. Butter the bread and lay it in a baking tray with the pigeon and the sauce. Grate some cheese over the sauce and let it cook in the oven for three to four hours. The "zuppa" in this case is not a soup but ought to have the consistency of a pie.*

Gallerie dell'Accademia

Five centuries of art in a collection containing innumerable masterpieces in the most important of Venice's galleries

The **Gallerie dell'Accademia**, one of the most important art galleries in Europe, occupies the site of the former **Chiesa della Carità** and the old **Lateran Convent**, a 16th Palladian building, and has assembled a noteworthy collection of works spanning five centuries of Veneto art.

In 1750 the Republic decided to set up an Academy for painters and sculptors which initially was directed by **Piazzetta** and then, later, by **Giovan Battista Tiepolo**. Works by the students of the Academy were gathered over the years and began forming the basis of an impressive collection of paintings and sculpture. At the beginning of the 19th century, the Academy moved to the gardens of **Palazzo Reale** near the present site and was soon enriched by the donations of many private collections. All the great Veneto artists are here represented as well as many foreign painters who have worked in Venice through the centuries.

Shopping for culinary treats

Venice's grocery shops are famous for the **pastas** they sell. This is no ordinary pasta, but pasta stuffed with an infinite variety of delicious fillings. Thus, you might want to try pasta with a filling of spinach, mixed herbs, salmon or even chocolate.

During the holiday season, Venice offers its own variation of the famous **panettone**. A locally-produced bottle of olive oil makes the perfect gift as does the excellent vinegar made in Belluno. The stores in Venice also sell fine mountain honeys.

The fruit liqueurs are another speciality worth trying. And no one should leave Venice without taking home at least one bottle of the famous Bassano **grappa.**

Above, left: *the* Ponte dell'Accademia. Above, center: *the entrance of the* Accademia *on the* Grand Canal. Left: *two masterpieces: the* Pietà, Titian's *last work and the* Island of San Giorgio *by* Francesco Guardi.

A review of the masterpieces

Trusting in the wisdom of the eye is the best rule for fully appreciating the wide spectrum of artistic masterpieces on display in the Galleria d'Accademia.

Let's begin with the 16th century Venetian painter **Giovanni Bellini** and his *Pietà*, a soft poignant depiction of an ageing *Madonna who carries Christ in a landscape* which perhaps combines elements of both Vicenza and Ravenna.

Slightly earlier is the stupendous *Madonna of the Zodiac* by **Cosmè Tura** whose soft though nervous style is clearly influenced by a mixture of Tuscan and northern European art.

The enigmatic *St Jerome and follower* by **Piero della Francesca** with its monumental figures is a masterpiece of perspective.

Painted in the first decade of the 16th century, **Lorenzo Lotto**'s *Portrait of a Gentleman* is distinguished by its dry cool tones and far removed from the subtle effects of light and shade which characterizes **Giorgione**'s large enigmatic painting, the *Tempest* (1507). This painting has been interpreted in many different ways, as a purely imaginative landscape, as a depiction of

Above, left to right: *the* Pietà *by* Bellini *(16th century); the* Madonna of the Zodiac, *so-called because of the astrological signs in the sky, by* Cosmè Tura *(1450);* St Jerome and a follower *by* Piero della Francesca *(1450);* St George, *small panel by* Andrea Mantegna *(1468).*

Center, left: The Tempest *by* Giorgione, *his enigmatic masterpiece (1507).*
Below: Banquet at the house of the Levi *by* Paolo Veronese *(1573).*

Left: *the* Miraculous Healing of a Madman, *one of the eight paintings in the* Miracles of the Reliquary *series by* Vittore Carpaccio *(1494).* Below: The English Ambassadors at the Court of Brittany, *again by* Vittore Carpaccio *(1495), a painting which forms part of one of the most important cycles of Venetian art in the 1400s.*

"Thebaid" or Venus suckling Cupid, according to the dictates of a 15th century novel. Heavily influenced by Florentine art is **Andrea Mantegna**'s *St George*, handsome in his armor despite the restrictive nature of the small panel. Mantegna had seen the works of **Donatello** and **Andrea del Castagno** and was probably influenced by them in his depiction of the saint who stands over the dead dragon. The 15th century comes to an end with the narrative art of **Vittore Carpaccio** whose *English Ambassadors at the Court of Brittany* is an admirable example of his work.

A century later, **Paolo Veronese**'s *Banquet at the house of the Levis* belongs to a completely different style of painting though without relinquishing the richness of setting and figurative design of his predecessors. Elegant and lively, **Gentile Bellini**'s *Procession of the Reliquary in Piazza San Marco* also provides us with a fascinating idea of the nature of San Marco's Basilica in those days.

Our journey through the centuries of Veneto art now brings us to the great Venetian *vedutisti*, such as **Canaletto** and **Francesco Guardi** whose vibrant and lyrical *the Island of San Giorgio* depicts a different but no less enchanting Venice.

Museo Correr

In the Ala Napoleonica in Piazza San Marco, this museum includes a section devoted to Venice's history, a picture gallery and a museum of the Risorgimento

The **Museo Correr** can be found in Piazza San Marco in the Ala Napoleonica. It was founded in 1830 thanks to the generous donation of **Theodore Correr** to the city and is interesting for a variety of reasons, not least of all the fine works of art it contains.

The museum is divided up into three sections in one of which Venice's history is documented, in another, the *Quadreria*, works of art are exhibited and finally the small museum dedicated to the Risorgimento. In the historical part of the museum there's the *Sala del Trono* which contains exhibits illustrating the role of the Duke and the procedures of his election, costumes of the era, images of the Bucintoro, the lavish boat of the Duke, the sea adventures of the Venetian Republic, an armory, various collections of old coins as well as documents relating to the arts, crafts, trades and games of the Venetians through history. However, the fulcrum of the museum is on the second floor and is constituted by the art gallery. Here are displayed a wide range of works, dating back to the Veneto-Byzantine artists and spanning the later centuries with works by **Lorenzo Veneziano**, the stupendous *Pietà* by **Cosmè Tura**, another *Pietà* by **Antonello da**

Below, left: The Courtesans by Vittore Carpaccio. Below, right: Portrait of the doge G. Mocenigo by Giovanni Bellini.

Messina, works by **Jacopo Bellini** (*Crucifixion*) and his sons **Gentile** (*Portrait of Doge Mocenigo*) and **Giovanni** (*Pietà*) and paintings by **Alvise Vivarini**. Other fine works on display here include **Lorenzo Lotto**'s splendid *Portrait of the Doge* and **Carpaccio**'s *the Courtesans*. There's also an early work by the sculptor **Antonio Canova** depicting *Daedalus and Icarus* which can be found in the historical section of the museum.

Clockwise: Crucifixion *by* Jacopo Bellini; Madonna with Child and St John *by* Bartolomeo Montagna; Dead Christ *by* Giovanni Bellini; Adoration of the Magi *by* Peter Bruegel; Pietà *by* Antonello da Messina.

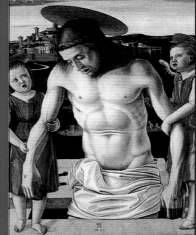

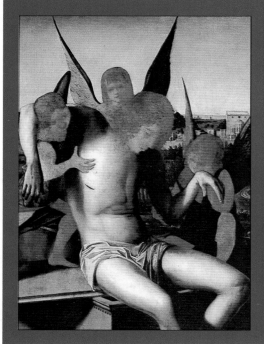

Glass, paper and masks: shopping in Venice

We have already alluded to the wide range of these specialized articles on sale in Venice's shops where **glass** objects in particular made by traditionally famous manufacturers such as Venini enjoy a widespread fame. The production of glass objects in the area has centuries of artisan tradition behind it and the articles on sale, including useful items such as wine glasses, bottles and all manner of lighting equipment, are made in a variety of original forms and colors which are as pleasing to the eye as they are practical.

The production of paper is another art in which Venice specializes, including the famous **carta marmorizzata** (marble-paper). This is made with the use of a gummy solution on which the varnish is then applied. Individual colors and styles are then chosen which provide agendas, notebooks and all manner of paper products with a refined and elegant look.

Masks are another speciality in which Venice excels and can be found in many shops, some of which are bona fide artistic workshops. Many of the masks produced are related to the *Commedia dell'Arte* though there are also a wide range of more modern masks with symbolic or abstract designs.

The triumph of Tintoretto

Scuola Grande di San Rocco

Three cycles of large paintings executed in the late 16th century which represent the artistic peak of the great Veneto painter

The **Scuola of San Rocco**, begun in 1517 and completed in 1560 by the architect **Bartolomeo Bon**, contains three stupendous cycles of large paintings which constitute the masterpieces of the artist **Jacopo Tintoretto**. The *Sala dell'Albergo* is where Tintoretto's great works can be found. His finest achievements include the large paintings dedicated to the *Passion - Christ before Pilate, the Crown of Thorns* and, at the center above the door, *Christ carrying the Cross*. His real masterpiece though is his *Crucifixion,* defined by one critic as an achievement of both material and spiritual immensity. The work is distinguished by its solid compositional structure in which Christ stands at the center isolated on the Cross from the gathering of figures around him. These works by Titian's pupil embody all the contradictions and ingenious flair of one of the world's greatest painters.

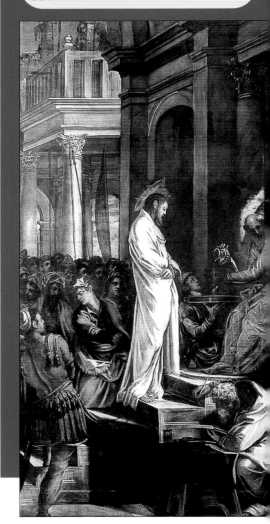

Two great cycles by Tintoretto: St Roch in prison comforted by an Angel *(detail)*. Below: Christ before Pilate.

Right: *A great masterpiece by* Jacopo Tintoretto: The Crucifixion (*two details*).
Below: Jacopo Tintoretto: The Last Supper.

Christ and Saints as depicted by a great 15th century painter

Scuola di San Giorgio: the masterpieces of Vittore Carpaccio

Vittore Carpaccio *at the* Scuola di San Giorgio: Triumph of St George, *detail.* Below: St Augustine *in his study.*

The **Scuola di San Giorgio degli Schiavoni**, also known as the **Scuola Dalmata** can be found on the Rio which divides the districts of San Francesco della Vigna and Santi Giovanni e Paolo. This is where Venice's Dalmation community lived after the first half of the 15th century. It was decorated in the following century with a splendid cycle of paintings by **Carpaccio** which any modern-day visitor to Venice should not miss the chance of witnessing first hand. The cycle represents episodes from the *Life of St George, Christ in the Garden, the Vocation of St Matthew, the Vision of St Augustine* and scenes from the *Life of St Jerome.*

All these works were executed between 1502 and 1507. In his *Legend of St George,* Carpaccio sets the life and adventures of the saint against an imaginative Oriental background with figures and costumes of a distinctly Eastern flavor. A magical air pervaded by a rich symphony of colors combines with a rather precise attention to detail in this picture.

In his *portrait of St Augustine,* Carpaccio has created a symbolic background with certain realistic touches to portray the Humanist dedicating himself to his studies. The face of the Saint is said to resemble the famous Greek scholar, Bessarione who donated the Libreria Marciana to Venice. A corner of the Orient also appears in the paintings depicting St Jerome.

Venetian life and culture in the 1800s

The Museo di Ca' Rezzonico: the splendor of 18th century Venice

Taking the vaporetto

On the Grand Canal, the Baroque **Palazzo Rezzonico**, once the home of the family to which it owes its name, was begun in 1649 by **Baldassarre Longhena** and completed in 1750 by **Giorgio Massari**. It was also once the home of the English poet Robert Browning. It now hosts a museum in which an image of the life of a noble Venetian family of the 18th century is recreated. Tapestries, lacquerwork, armchairs typical of the period, ornate furniture and precious ornaments all combine, above all in the *Sala da Ballo* on the first floor, to recreate the refined elegance which characterized the cultural life of the nobility in 18th century Venice.

There is also here a reconstruction of the **Villa del Tiepolo** with the chiaroscuro frescoes executed for the family villa in 1753 by the son of Giovan Battista Tiepolo, **Gian Domenico**. Also fascinating is the tiny theater of the era, reconstructed with its puppets and the old **Farmacia di San Stin**.

The **Museo Rezzonico** is also notable for the fine paintings it contains of all the major Venetian artists of the 18th century, including works by **Rosalba Carriera**, **Tiepolo**, **Longhi** and **Canaletto**.

The **vaporetto**, a large diesel-propelled boat, is Venice's principle and most economical mode of transport (the alternative is provided by the **motoscafi**, river taxis which are comparatively expensive). The main line of the vaporetti naturally runs up and down the Grand Canal. They travel at a leisurely speed, allowing the passenger to take in all the marvellous sights provided by the canal and its backdrop. On certain lines the vaporetti are replaced by faster **motoscafi pubblici** (motorboats). There are also the **traghetti** which are a particular kind of gondola for those who want to cross the Grand Canal at certain points. There are also services which, at fixed times of the day, connect mainland Venice to its islands.

Sequence of 18th century Venetian furniture at Ca' Rezzonico. Clockwise: bureau, armchairs and console table.

Out and about among the canals, bridges and small squares

Many-faceted Venice: behind every corner a surprise

Having seen the monuments, the palaces, the churches and museums, this city still has much to offer in terms of visual beauty and intrigue.

We take here a rapid look at a few of the not so famous sights worth seeing and other collections of works of art not previously mentioned in these pages.

Two large marble lions stand at the entrance to the *Arsenale* which once graced the ships of the maritime Republic. The *Museo Storico Navale*, containing images of Venice's history through the centuries, is also the home of the last Bucintoro.

The Riva degli Schiavoni (in the two photos on the right) *runs along the basin of San Marco as far as the gardens where a part of the* Biennale d'Arte *takes place.*

Ponte della Paglia *(Bridge of Straw – see photo on the right), a 14th century construction which owes its name to the fact that boats carrying straw for the prisoners moored here, is one of the best places in Venice to take picturesque photos.*

Though tiny, Harry's Bar enjoys great fame in Venice. It was a favorite haunt of the American writer Ernest Hemingway (see photo below) and remains to this day a lively meeting place for locals and foreigners alike.

In Palazzo Venier dei Leoni *one can find the Guggenheim collection which, thanks to the collaboration of the Guggenheim Museum in New York, boasts the best collection of modern art in Venice. The work of many of the great artists of the 20th century can be admired here –* Picasso, Magritte, De Chirico, Duchamp, Brancusi, Leger, Braque, Chagall, Pollock, Mirò, Mondrian *and others.*

The *Hotel Danieli*, one of the most renowned and historical hotels of the city which stands on the famous Riva degli Schiavoni.

The Giudecca (see photo on the left) *is a long narrow island in a world of its own and hosts a number of youth hostels. It was here that Palladio built the extraordinary* Chiesa del Redentore.

Veneto cuisine: recipes

Rice dishes

RICE AND PEAS (RISI E BISI). Fry the bacon cut up into pieces in a pan with an onion, butter and olive oil. Add the peas and cook for fifteen minutes. In another saucepan boil the husks of the peas, drain them and then boil them again, adding a consommé made with half a beef stock cube and the rice. Then add the already prepared bacon and pea sauce and occasionally stir. Cook over a low flame and add a little salt. When the rice is cooked serve with parsley and lots of grated parmesan cheese.

INGREDIENTS (SERVES FOUR). 300 grams of peas; 200 grams of rice; bacon; onion; butter; olive oil; salt; parsley; parmesan cheese and a stock cube.

RISOTTO WITH MUSSELS (RISOTTO CON PEOCI). Clean the mussels well and place them in a frying pan with a little olive oil and a clove of garlic and cook until the mussels open. Extract them from their shells, put them on a plate and pour the liquid from the pan over them. Place in a pan a little butter, two tablespoons of olive oil and an onion. Add the rice, moistening it with hot water in which dissolve a fish stock cube and cook for twenty minutes. Before the rice is properly cooked, add the mussels and their liquid, a little pepper and a little butter.

INGREDIENTS (SERVES FOUR). 400 grams of rice; 800 grams of mussels; olive oil; garlic; butter; onion; pepper and a fish stock cube.

RISOTTO WITH SAUSAGE (RISI E LU-GANEGHE). Sauté a little butter and ham fat and add the turnips sliced into cubes and the sausages (luganega are the famous sausages from Treviso). After a minute or so add half a glass of white wine. When the wine has been absorbed add two liters of water with beef or chicken stock. When this boils, add the rice and stir occasionally until cooked. Serve with parsley and grated parmesan cheese.

INGREDIENTS (SERVES FOUR). 150 grams of sausages; 150 grams of rice; 100 grams of turnips; ham fat; onion; butter; wine; beef or chicken stock; parsley and parmesan cheese.

RICE SOUP WITH PUMPKIN (MINESTRA DE RISO CO LA SUCA). Peel the pumpkin and remove pips before cooking in salted water. Add a little butter and milk to the pulp of the pumpkin and stir. Cook the rice separately in salted water. When half cooked pour in the pumpkin sauce and finish cooking over a low flame and add a little salt.

INGREDIENTS (SERVES FOUR). 300 grams of yellow pumpkin; 150 grams of rice; 50 grams of butter; milk and salt.

Beach resort and worldly cultural center

Lido di Venezia,
history, high society and a famous beach

A residential suburb of Venice endowed with a wonderful beach, the **Isola del Lido** is connected to mainland Venice by a vaporetto service. In the 19th century it was a favorite haunt of artists and poets like **Byron** and **Shelley** and soon became, thanks to its elegant hotels, one of the most renowned beach resorts in Europe.

It was also made famous by **Thomas Mann**'s "Death in Venice" and the subsequent film of the novel by **Visconti**.

Viale Santa Maria Elisabetta is lined with elegant designer shops and famous hotels include the Excelsior and Des Bains. There are also several Liberty-style churches and buildings on the island.

The film festival and the Biennale d'Arte

A hundred years of international cinema and figurative arts

Between August and September Venice annually hosts the **International Film Festival** *which, since 1932 when it was inaugurated during the fascist regime, continues to hold its place as one of the most important celebrations of cinema in the world. Every year a jury of experts sit through a wide selection of movies from all over the globe while famous celebrities from the world of the arts converge on the* **Palazzo del Cinema** *and the* **Astra on the Lido** *in a huge celebration of the Movie industry.*

The periodic culmination of the lively artistic activity in Venice, where art exhibitions, often of an international nature, are always plentiful, is represented by the **Biennale d'Arte** *which organizes shows of contemporary and avant-guard art in many fields including Theater, Music and Architecture. Founded in 1885, the Biennale takes place between June and September in odd years and in a variety of locations, including the public gardens and the Arsenale. Artists and works from more than 40 countries are represented and it is one of the most important festivals of its kind in the world.*

Thousand-year-old churches blazing with gold backgrounds

Older than Venice,
Torcello preserves stupendous Byzantine mosaics

The **island of Torcello**, which today has less than a hundred inhabitants, might almost be considered the mother of Venice since it was from here that the city of canals took form and came to life.

Now little more than a lonely cluster of houses huddled around its picturesque piazza, Torcello nevertheless contains an important religious complex constituted by the **Baptistery** and **Cathedral of Santa Maria Assunta** which dates back to 639, though it was enlarged in the 11th century.

The dazzling interior consists of three aisles flanked by a double row of nine columns and contains a solemn bishop's thrown, a *sarcophagus* preserving the remains of *St Heliodorus* and a splendid mosaic floor.

On the internal walls of the façade can be found the cathedral's most impressive feature, another cycle of mosaics probably executed by craftsmen from Constantinople depicting the *Last Judgement* and the *Virgin with Child*. Nearby, stands the small **church of Santa Fosca**, built at the beginning of the 11th century.

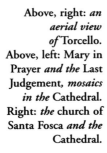

Above, right: *an aerial view of* Torcello. Above, left: Mary in Prayer *and the* Last Judgement, *mosaics in the* Cathedral. Right: *the* church of Santa Fosca *and the* Cathedral.

*A few minutes
from Venice by boat*

Murano, home of Vivarini and a world center of glass and glaziers

Very near to Venice (a few minutes by boat), **Murano** is the famous home of glass. Built on five small islands and divided by a canal with only one bridge, Murano is medieval in origin and was soon assimilated by Venice and thus adopted its styles and colors. The glassworks were moved from Venice to Murano at the beginning of the 14th century where they have continued to flourish to this very day. Highly skilled craftsmen producing exquisite artistic glass articles now work on the island for world famous companies such as Venini, Barovier & Toso and Seguso.

The factories where these splendid examples of the art of glassmaking are produced – bottles, vases, glasses, candelabra, statues and just about anything else transparent or colored glass can be modelled into forming – all welcome visitors. There's also a glass museum – **Museo dell'Arte Vetraria** – in the 17th century **Palazzo Giustinian**.

The beautiful 14th century **church of San Pietro Martire** is well worth a visit as it contains works by **Giovanni Bellini**, **Palma il Giovane** and **Paolo Veronese** as is the **Basilica of Santi Maria e Donato**, a fine example of Veneto-Byzantine architecture, and the **Palazzo Da Mula**.

The other islands of the lagoon

Other sights worth taking in on the lagoon include the **isoletta di San Lazzaro degli Armeni**, that houses a large religious which is more than nine centuries old. Here there's an art gallery, a museum and a splendid library as well as the peacocks in the cloisters of the monks.

Among the 34 small islands, the small island known as **San Francesco nel Deserto** is also worth visiting. It was donated to the Franciscans in 1228 and is still inhabited by the order today. It has a small church, two fine cloisters and a beautiful garden surrounded by the sea.

Examples of glass objects made in Murano.
Above left: *aerial view of Murano.*
Below: *the* church of Santa Maria.

Boats, the brightly-colored homes of fishermen and an enchanted landscape

Burano: four small islands renowned for the art of lace-making

Above: a panoramic view of Burano. Right, above: Filippo De Pisis, the Veneto painter who has painted Murano countless times. Below: a lace stall.

Burano, about ten kilometers from Venice, is one of the most famous islands in the Venetian lagoon. Already a flourishing community in the 14th century, it is composed of four small islands which are connected by a series of bridges. It's a charming little fishing village enlivened by its brightly-colored houses and multitude of boats.

Its fame however, besides the beauty of its landscapes, resides in its long tradition in the art of lace-making which began as far back as the 16th century and was revived towards the end of the 1800s.

Today, lace-making is still a thriving industry on the island and there's a school and a museum dedicated to the art which can be found next to **Palazzo Podestà**.

The 16th century **church of San Martino** contains a *Crucifixion* by **Giovan Battista Tiepolo** (1725).

Veneto cuisine: recipes

Main courses

LIVER ALLA VENEZIANA (FEGATO AL-LA VENEZIANA). *Sauté some olive oil and butter in a frying pan then add parsley and onion and fry for three quarters of an hour. Now add the liver flavored with a meat sauce or a consommé. When the liver is cooked, which does not take long, salt it and place on a serving dish and arrange around the borders toasted bread. The dish might then be served with mashed potato.*

INGREDIENTS (SERVES FOUR). 600 grams of calves' liver; 500 grams of onion; 60 grams of olive oil; 30 grams of butter; stock cube or meat sauce; parsley; salt and toasted bread.

TURKEY ALLA SCHIAVONA (DINDO AL-LA SCHIAVONA). *Fill the turkey with six raw chestnuts and a few dried prunes soaked in warm water and add chopped celery and a little salt. Dress the turkey with stringed slices of bacon and cook slowly on a spit, using the juice from the meat to help brown the turkey. Serve with french fries.*

INGREDIENTS (SERVES EIGHT). 1 young turkey; 6 chestnuts; 8 dried prunes; 100 grams of bacon; celery and salt.

TRIPE ALLA TREVISANA (TRIPPA ALLA TREVISANA). *Sauté a little butter, a little lard and a sliced onion. Add the tripe together with a little rosemary. Cook for a short while then add half a liter of stock and simmer for half an hour. Serve the tripe with slices of toasted bread and a generous serving of grated parmesan cheese.*

INGREDIENTS (SERVES FOUR). 1kg of tripe; lard; onion; butter; rosemary; toasted bread and parmesan cheese.

FRIED FROG (RANE FRITTE). *Detach the legs of the frogs, cover them in olive oil, salt, pepper, lemon juice and parsley and let sit for at least half an hour. Cover the frogs in breadcrumbs and fry in an abundance of boiling olive oil. Drain on absorbent paper and serve hot. An alternative way of preparing this dish is to dip the frogs in a mixture of flour, beaten eggs and breadcrumbs, following afterwards the same procedure as above.*

INGREDIENTS (SERVES FOUR). 700 grams of skinned frog; olive oil; salt; pepper; breadcrumbs; lemon juice; parsley or, alternatively, beaten eggs and flour.

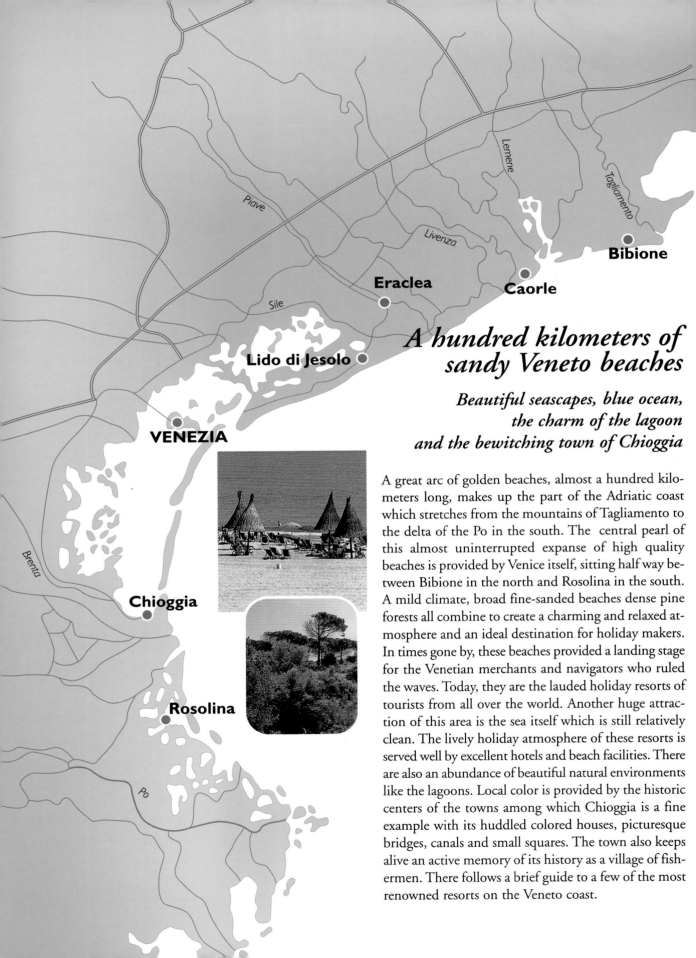

Lemene

Tagliamento

Piave

Livenza

Bibione

Eraclea

Sile

Caorle

Lido di Jesolo

A hundred kilometers of sandy Veneto beaches

Beautiful seascapes, blue ocean, the charm of the lagoon and the bewitching town of Chioggia

VENEZIA

Brenta

Chioggia

Rosolina

Po

A great arc of golden beaches, almost a hundred kilometers long, makes up the part of the Adriatic coast which stretches from the mountains of Tagliamento to the delta of the Po in the south. The central pearl of this almost uninterrupted expanse of high quality beaches is provided by Venice itself, sitting half way between Bibione in the north and Rosolina in the south. A mild climate, broad fine-sanded beaches dense pine forests all combine to create a charming and relaxed atmosphere and an ideal destination for holiday makers. In times gone by, these beaches provided a landing stage for the Venetian merchants and navigators who ruled the waves. Today, they are the lauded holiday resorts of tourists from all over the world. Another huge attraction of this area is the sea itself which is still relatively clean. The lively holiday atmosphere of these resorts is served well by excellent hotels and beach facilities. There are also an abundance of beautiful natural environments like the lagoons. Local color is provided by the historic centers of the towns among which Chioggia is a fine example with its huddled colored houses, picturesque bridges, canals and small squares. The town also keeps alive an active memory of its history as a village of fishermen. There follows a brief guide to a few of the most renowned resorts on the Veneto coast.

● BIBIONE

Bibione can trace back its origins to antiquity. Archaeological digs have uncovered the remains of Roman villas beneath the town. For a long time however it remained a deserted and solitary place until, in fact, very recently when its beaches were discovered by tourists and all of a sudden an abundance of hotels, sports centers and swimming pools sprang up. However, all this tourist activity has not diminished the tranquility of the location with its vast stretches of golden sand (seven kilometers of beach), its large pine forests and its long line of fishing valleys.

Bibione is easily reached, served both by the Venice-Trieste-Udine autostrada and the railway line from Venice to Trieste.

● CAORLE

An old Roman port, at the mouth of the river Livenza, Caorle is today both a lively town of fishermen and a renowned tourist attraction. The very old **Cathedral**, built around the 11th century has three aisles with alternating columns and pillars. The **Campanile**, made of brick, is attractive. The town's

small harbor with its flotsam of fishing boats is extremely picturesque and can accommodate up to seven hundred boats. The town is also justifiably proud of its restaurants where one can eat extremely well and in a beautiful setting. Leisure activities offered by Caorle include mini golf and tennis as well as a boat and motorboat hiring service.

Caorle: the large beach and the dam with the Chiesa-Faro.
Above: a lively sandy beach on the Adriatic Coast.

Lagoons, fishing and "casoni"

The "casoni" are provisional homesteads which provide the fishermen of the area with a dwelling place during the fishing season. Until very recently, fishing was the area's principle source of income. A profusion of these rustic and elegant buildings line the lagoons of the coast, some not far from Caorle, and, in some cases, have survived in tact and are still upheld out of respect for their tradition. They are built on stilts embedded in the ground which are bound with rushes and covered by reeds.

Eating by the sea

The Veneto Riviera is renowned not only for its coasts, its good climate and the beauty of its scenery but also for the high quality of its cuisine. Pride of place, not surprisingly, is given to seafood dishes featuring eels, scampi and grilled gilthead. Favorite wines include *Tocai, Merlot* and *Cabernet*. In Chioggia, favorite dishes include various risottos and pumpkin.

The Veneto Riviera hosts many seasonal food fairs including the *Sagra del Pesce* (fish) in Ferragosto and the *Sagra dell'Uva* (grape) in September.

● *ERACLEA MARE*

Thus is called the splendid coastal zone around the town of Eraclea which was once a Roman settlement.

It can be reached by road or by taking a train to Donà di Piave.

The coast, stretching from Caorle to the mouth of the River Piave, is more than five kilometers long and, in large part, is flanked by lush pinewoods which mix their sweet scent with the smell of the sea.

This area is especially popular with campers and is also endowed with many holiday villages dotted among the pines.

● *LIDO DI JESOLO*

Lido di Jesolo can be found between Faro del Cavallino and the mouth of the River Piave. It is one of the chief beach resorts on the Adriatic thanks to the fine gold nature of its beaches and all the sporting facilities it offers. In fact, here you'll find an enormous variety of leisure activities including a wealth of tennis courts, minigolf, go kart racing, water skiing, windsurfing, motor boats and horse-riding schools. But neither has Lido di Jesolo lost the tranquil historical atmosphere it has possessed since antiquity, for it possesses a history which goes back over a thousand years. Suffering defeat at the hands of the Franks before the year 1000, it then remained under Venetian rule for centuries.

Eraclea Mare, between Piave and Caorle, offers five kilometers of sandy beaches and pinewoods.

The strange lagoon-like structure of Lido di Jesolo, whose sands originate from the Dolomites.

● *CHIOGGIA, THE SPELL OF A TINY VENICE*

Chioggia consists of four small parallel rectangular islands connected by bridges while another long bridge connects the town to the mainland.

Chioggia is a kind of Venice in miniature in that it mirrors the structure and effect of its illustrious cousin.

Less solemn than Venice, it is nevertheless graced by the same bewitching network of canals winding their way alongside the brightly colored houses which are specially designed to accommodate the boats.

The stone 17th century bridge **Ponte Vigo** offers a panoramic view of the canals and its traffic of fishing boats which are known locally as *bragozzi*. Because of the good-natured character of its inhabitants, Chioggia was chosen by the great 18th century dramatist **Goldoni** as the setting for his play, *Le Baruffe Chiozzotte*.

The **Cathedral**, **Palazzo Comunale**, the **Granaio Pubblico** and the **Chiesa di Sant'Andrea** are all well worth visiting.

After Chioggia, continuing along the coast, you come to Rosolina Mare, a nine kilometer-stretch of wide sandy beaches.

We have now almost reached the spellbinding Delta del Po.

Two images of the picturesque Chioggia. Above: the balustrade of the Canale Perottolo.

Lacemakers and "chiozota e broeto"

Having enjoyed the sights of this vibrant fishing town – the medieval Palazzo Comunale, *the* Madonna of Sansovino *and the* polyptych *by* Paolo Veneziano *– you might like to pay a visit to its shops and restaurants. Chioggia boasts a long tradition in the art of lacemaking and the craft is still practiced today. In the summer, it hosts a famous fish fair. Specialities served up on Chioggia's dining tables include pumpkin dishes,* risoto *and "chiozota e broeto".*

For those with a taste for literature, it's worth reading Carlo Goldoni's *depiction of the good-natured people of Chioggia in his splendid comedy "Le Baruffe chiozzotte".*

ROVIGO

At the heart of the Polesine, a fervid agricultural market, Rovigo was a medieval town (it still preserves the remains) which fell under Venetian rule and then, in the 1800s, was governed by Austria. It is endowed with many churches and palaces and boasts many artistic masterpieces.

Flora and fauna in the enchanting landscapes of the Polesine.

Rovigo provides its attentive visitor with three particular treats: the first consists of all its medieval remains complete with impressive towers and walls; the second is the **Pinacoteca** with its lavish collection of paintings from Italy and abroad; the third is **Piazza Vittorio Emanuele II**, the heart of the city, with its impressive historical buildings and its warm

The Polesine, ancient plain between two rivers

*Here we find ourselves in a vast and ancient plain, an evocative landscape bounded by two rivers, the **Adige** and the **Po**, furrowed by a hundred navigable canals, populated by waterbirds including the great heron and the bittern, near the great delta of Italy's principle river, the Po where once upon a time history was made. In fact, Adria, today a working town, once played the role of the most important port in the entire Adriatic. Nowadays, the most interesting places to visit are those around **Porto Tolle**, where it's possible to hire a bike and cross the beautiful natural splendour of this oasis or rent a canoe to explore the network of canals. Here, at the beginning of the fifties, the Po overflowed and caused a terrible flood which decimated many villages and left homeless almost two hundred thousand people. The most important city of the Polesine region is the nearby Rovigo.*

Rovigo: Piazza Vittorio Emanuele II *surrounded by impressive buildings dating from the 15th to the 20th centuries.*

convivial atmosphere. Piazza Vittorio Emanuele II is the center of the city: large, spacious, open-planned but at the same time a domestic and homey square at the heart of the city. Overlooked by the tall granite column of Istria with the Venetian lion perched on its tip, the piazza houses the beautiful **Torre dell'Orologio** and the old **Loggia dei Notai** – daily meeting place of the town council – with its elegant three arched arcade and collection of paintings on the first floor. The Piazza also houses the noble **Palazzo dell'Accademia dei Concordi**, constructed in the 18th century by **Sante Baseggio**, faced by the **Palazzo Rovarella**, an old pawnbrokers which still retains traces of its 14th century origins. Other impressive palaces in Rovigo include the 17th century **Palazzo Angeli**, in the road of the same name and the **Palazzo Roncale** (in via Laurenti) built by the sanmicheli in the 1500s.

On the menu, fresh water fish and good wine

On the menus of Rovigo and its environs, Veneto cuisine draws on the influence of its neighbour, Emilia, perhaps the region of Italy which takes the most delight in food. Therefore, fine lasagnes and tortellinis are served up here. Of their own, Rovigo cuisine consists principally of fresh water fish dishes, served fried or boiled. Well worth trying are the flambe eels *(a cheap dish but immensely tasty),* arzavole roasted on a spit, *or the excellent* sturgeon caviar *from the Po. It also goes without saying that you won't be dissatisfied if you order any of the typical specialities of the area –* pasta with white beans, risi and bisi, tagliatelle with truffles *and "bondola" which is a delicious pork-based dish. As for your glass, fill it with* Merlot *or* Cabernet, *rich wines which are the fruit of Veneto's fertile soil.*

Left to right: *the unfinished façade of the* Duomo *of Rovigo and the 16th century* church of San Bartolomeo. Below: *the* Presentation of the Virgin at the Temple *by Francesco Maffei. The painting is preserved in the* church of the Beata Vergine del Soccorso *known as the "La Rotonda".*

Nobody should leave Rovigo without having seen the collection of paintings from the Venetian school displayed in the **Accademia dei Concordi**. They range from the 15th to the 19th century and include works by **Giovanni Bellini**, **Dosso Dossi**, **Sebastiano Mazzoni**, **Luca Giordano**, **Giambattista Piazzetta**, **Giovan Battista Tiepolo** and the great female painter, **Rosalba**. Not to be missed are the 17th century Flemish tapestries inspired by the *Triumphs* of the poet **Francesco Petrarch**.

Another collection of art which demands to be seen is in the **Pinacoteca del Seminario** (via Tre Martiri 89) where the Venetian school is once again well-represented with works by Luca Giordano, Giovanbattista Piazzetta and the beautiful *Contadinello* by **Pietro Longhi**.

The history of this land in a museum

Whoever pays a visit to Rovigo would do well, in order to enter into the spirit and atmosphere of this region, to stop off at the Museo Civico della Civiltà in Polesine *which reconstructs the history of this unique and evocative area, also from a naturalistic and ethnographic point of view. The museum has archaeological rooms containing artefacts from both the Bronze and Iron ages found in Fratta Polesine which date back to 11 and 1000 B.C. as well as rooms displaying artefacts from the Roman period. The naturalistic and ethnographic section is well worth investigating where the customs and ways of life of the countryside and the artisans in the 19th and early 20th century are well documented. There are in fact many small museums in these parts which recount the history of the town or village in which they can be found and all warrant a visit.*

Adria's Teatro Comunale. Below: *a ritual vase in the form of a horse in Adria's* Museo Archeologico Nazionale.

Adria, a slice of history
To begin with, the principle port of the Adriatic, now a mainland city, in the heart of the Polesine, it retains the vestiges of many civilisations

Nature and history merge in an evocative union which stretches back into the distant recesses of time and place. It was Adria, it would seem, which gave its name to the Adriatic sea when it was the sea's principle port; then the sea receded and Ravenna took over Adria's role. Adria was, in turns, a Syracusan colony, a Roman municipality, under Byzantine rule and then taken under the wing of the omnipresent Venezian Republic. Its terrain was then altered by a rich network of canals and recent redevelopment and drainage: today, the Bacino di Canalbianco retains an impressive environmental charm.

A large part of Adria's surviving, many-faceted past resides in the two adjacent churches – the **Cattedrale Nuova** and the **Cattedrale Vecchia**. The latter houses a marble baptismal font and a crypt as well as Byzantine frescoes from the 7th century and the remains of a terracotta altar attributed to the 15th century artist **Michele da Firenze**. The 19th century Cattedrale Nuova on the otherhand is dedicated to the saints Peter and Paul and possesses a nave with two aisles and an older Baroque *campanile*.

Among the precious works to be found inside there's a 6th-century Byzantine bas-relief from Ephesus and, in the sacristy, a Byzantine crucifix perhaps originating from Crete.

In the basin of the Canalbianco, with its strong Venetian flavor, we find side by side the **Comunale Theater of G.B. Scarpari** and the **church of Sant'Andrea** which flaunts a 15th century stone *Ecce Homo* on its portal.

Another of Adria's splendours is the **Basilica di Santa Maria Assunta della Tomba**, an old church which up until the 18th century had been restored and altered many times and was again overhauled in the 20th century and which contains many valuable works of art including a high relief *Dormitio Virginis* in terracotta attribuited to **Michele da Firenze**; an octagonal *baptismal font* from the 8th century and a medieval holy water font in marble.

In the municipal Pinacoteca building, Adria houses more treasures – to mention but a few, there's some bronzes of **Pisanello** and the *portrait of the blind man of Adria*, the 16th century masterpiece of **Tintoretto**.

That chariot, those cavalry

The glory of the many past civilisations of this land can be observed in the splendid collections of the important **National Archaeological Museum** in via Badini. From remote times there are vases and ceramics from the Iron age, Etruscan artifacts, Greek bronzes and gold treasures from Roman times; you'll also find household goods from the paleovenetian civilisations neighboring the Adria of antiquity as well as pottery and funeral and votive figurines found in the surrounding necropolises. But the most evocative feeling is perhaps to be found in front of the mile post of via Popilia, now contained in the courtyard, which bears one of the oldest latin epigraphs of northern Italy. Then there's the impressive famous **tomb of the Celtic** or Veneto warrior according to the chariot because it contained three skeletons and the remains of a cart. All of which makes a trip to Adria well worth the effort.

Where a great river meets the sea, in one of the most bewitching parks in Europe

Rosolina

Po

On the Delta of the Po

Lagoons, pools, dunes, sandbanks and an immense wildlife made up of herons, coots and teals. Already immense after the mouth of the Po was deviated by the Venetians in the 1600s, it is now the most vast and interesting Italian zones and that is to be found between the mouths of the rivers Adige and Reno

The National Park

Below: two typical landscapes of the Delta del Po.

The **National Park**, one of the most interesting in Europe, includes the strip of the delta between the Adriatic sea and the Romea highway.

A large part of the park is made up of a vast coastland with lagoons and valleys.

The park also extends into the Emilia region with the Comacchio valleys. The park includes several branches of the Po (Po di Levante, Po di Maistra, Po Grande, Po di Tolle, Po di Gnocca, Po di Goro), while to the south there are only vast areas of marshland.

A unique landscape in the world

Sometimes wild, sometimes domesticated by man, formed by vegetation and water, the landscape of the Po Delta, combining all manner of natural wonders, casts an unfailing spell over the visitor: the benches and the dunes, the living lagoons and the coves, the sandbank zones and the valleys. The vegetation too is varied and sometimes submerged.

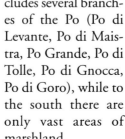

Aerial view of the Delta zona.
Below, left to right: *the Delta region boasts a rich variety of wildlife. No less rich is the cuisine of the area, specializing in fish-based dishes.*

Places to visit

It contains so many beautiful landscapes that the Delta is an ideal place to just wander about in at your leisure, going wherever the mood takes you, among the dunes, along the waterways, looking up every so often at the impressive flocks of birds taking to the air. However there are specific places which demand to be seen: **Contarina**, **Taglio di Po**, **Lendinara** and **Porto Tolle** for example. Close by Porto Tolle, the island of **Donzella**, the largest of the archipelago, is well worth a visit. From Porto Tolle, an excursion can be made into the southern part of the Delta. **Scardovari**, a fishing village and a fish farming market, is especially picturesque. There's also the exhibition of the life of the farming community in Porto Tolle.

A rich variety of birds

The Delta is characterized by a rich and varied wildlife, especially indigenous and migratory birds – the sea pie, the plover, the coot, the garganey, the teal, the dun-bird. Especially impressive are the red heron, the ash-grey heron, the little egret, the bittern and the night heron. They all dip their beaks in the water among the pools, swamps and dunes or take to the air in brief, thick packs in a naturalistic spectacle of rare beauty.

Good swamp food

Fish, better if from a river, is the centerpiece of the table: here you'll be able to sample **Risotto di branzino** *(bass), rice in a fish stock and* **Broeto** *(a fish soup). Second courses are dominated by eel: well worth trying are the boiled octopus (***Bisato in tecia***), roasted flambe eel and fried or boiled fresh water fish. The cat fish is especially delicious. Other typical dishes include duck, teal roasted on a spit and baccala. Also a treat in itself is the* **Granseola**, *a large crab found in the Adriatic.*

PADUA

Cultured thanks to its historic university, religious thanks to its cult of Sant'Antonio, beautiful thanks to its masterpieces by Donatello, Giotto and many others.

Splendid city of Giotto and del Santo

Above: *panorama of the city of* Padua. Right: *portrait of the artist* Giotto *and an image of* Sant'Antonio, *venerated in this city.*

The vibrant young population who attend Padua University, one of the oldest in the world (it dates back to the 13th century); the universally recognized canonization of Saint Anthony to whom the famous **Basilica del Santo** was erected; the stupendous masterpieces of two artists, Giotto and Donatello (both of whom were in fact Tuscan and not Paduan) – these are some of the things which make Padua such a lively, compelling and prestigious city, rich in cultural assets. Padua is a very old city. It was once a palaeo-Venetic settlement many centuries before the birth of Christ. It later became an important Roman colony and the great historian Titus Livy was born within its walls. Around the beginning of the 13th century, a group of students and

professors founded the university and the splendid **Basilica di Sant'Antonio** was raised. At this time Padua enjoyed a period of political freedom. Then came a brief spell of dictatorship when the city fell under the iron fist of Ezzelino da Romano. It was then incorporated into the Venice Republic where it was to remain until the end of the 1800s when it fell briefly to the French before succumbing to Habsburg rule until the unification of Italy. With the passing of the centuries Padua has collected a formidable bounty of art masterpieces – the sublime *Cappella degli Scrovegni* frescoes by **Giotto** spring immediately to mind as well as those by **Giusto de' Menabuoi** in the **Baptistery** and those by **Altichiero Veronese**.

> ### NOT TO BE MISSED
> ● *Small and charming, there are certain sights in Padua, linked to its cultural and religious heritage, which have to be experienced in order to enter into the spirit of the city. The entire city revolves around the* Basilica del Santo *and thus is our first port of call. Then we move onto the* Cappella degli Scrovegni *containing the frescoes by* Giotto *which constitute a pivotal moment in the development of Western art. Finally, we make our way to Piazza Santo, dominated by the* Equestrian Statue of Gattamelata, *and visit the* Basilica *where Donatello's masterpieces are to be found.*

Above: *the* equestrian statue of Gattamelata *by* Donatello *in* Padua.

Padua's piazzas

*The piazzas "dei Signori", "delle Erbe" and "dei Frutti"
are the places where one comes face to face with art, history and the vibrancy
of daily life in Padua. From the splendor of "Palazzo della Ragione" to the
elegant "Loggia della gran Guardia", a series of masterpieces enlivened by the
bustle of the street markets*

Like other cities in Veneto, the squares in Padua too are the locations where art, history and the lively ebb and flow of daily life all converge. Three piazzas, very close to one another, form the core of Padua's life: Piazza dei Signori, Piazza delle Erbe and Piazza dei Frutti. All three boast monuments of high artistic achievement.

Soaring up in the vicinity of all three squares, stands the magnificent **Palazzo della Ragione**. This stunning building which dates back to 1218-18 was built to house Padua's law courts. The ground floor, looking out on the piazza, is endowed with two levels of arcades and hosted a number of workshops. From the arcades, one climbs an outside stairway and enters the long loggia which runs along the façade of the building. This in turn gives way to what was probably the largest enclosed space in medieval Europe, an immense and stunning hall measuring 80 meters long and 27 meters wide. It was origi-

Above: Piazza dei Signori, *the heart of Padua.* **Below:** *the* **Loggia della Gran Guardia.**

In Piazza dei Signori, *the* Palazzo del Capitanio *and the* Torre dell'Orologio. *Below: the* Church of San Clemente.

nally decorated in frescoes by Giotto but the work of this great artist was destroyed by the great fire which devastated the palace in 1420. Other artists have played a part in decorating the vast sweep of these walls both before and after Giotto, including **Giusto de' Menabuoi**, whose *Allegories and Saints* occupies the lower part of the hall and was executed at the end of the 1300s and managed to survive the blaze. The second section is divided up into no less than 333 paintings and covers three sides of the hall. These were painted by **Niccolò Moretto** and depict astrological subjects – a true bible of the stars referring to the nature and fate of man in relation to the movements and conjunctions

of the stars on their monthly rounds.

There's also an enormous wooden horse in the hall modelled on Donatello's celebrated Gattamelata and which was made in 1466 to be used as part of a jousting tournament during public festivals. Another curious artefact in the hall is the so-called *Pietra of Vituperio* where, once upon a time, bankrupt Paduans were put in the stocks before being exiled.

The exterior of the Palazzo also warrants close inspection. The entire building, structured in a rhomboidal form, is positioned in such a way as to allow the rays of the sun to enter through the myriad windows and illuminate the frescoes of the zodiac signs at the appropriate moment, hence in January the sun lights up Aires

and so on and so forth. The palace is crowned by great ship's-keel roof. The arcaded façade looks out onto two squares, Piazza delle Erbe and Piazza della Frutta which hosts a bustling street market, and thus participates in the busy daily life of the city. A wealth of other historical palaces stand around or very near Piazza delle Erbe including **Palazzo degli Anziani**, the **Torre degli Anziani** and **Palazzo del Consiglio** which together more or less form a single complex.

Palazzo degli Anziani, built in 1285, has a portico and has been altered through the centuries (the old mullioned windows with two lights were turned into rectangular windows – though have now been restored to their original state – and a third floor was added, increasing the height of the building). The **Palazzo del Podestà** was restructured by **Andrea Moroni** in the 1500s – a long balustrade along the façade separates the ground and first floor. The tall, almost entirely window-less Torre del Comune or degli Anziani has now had its sober medieval look restored to it after recent restoration. The Palazzo del Consiglio, standing on the lively Piazza della Frutta, was built in 1283 of Istria stone and Greek marble and is ennobled by a cornice running along its façade. Let's move now to the principle square in Padua, Piazza dei Signori. Here, the **Palazzo del Capitano** dominates the entire side of the

The "Pietra of Vituperio" and, above, a detail from a fresco, both in the splendid **Palazzo della Ragione** *(above).*
Left: *a view of* Piazza delle Erbe.

square. It was the old home of Padua's judiciary and its façade was re-fashioned during the 1500s and today is subdivided up into three orders. At the center of the Palazzo rises a triumphal arch, altered by Falconetto in 1523, which acts as an entrance; above on the tower sits the beautiful clock dating back to 1437. On the east side of the square, the medieval **Chiesa di San Clemente** is one of the oldest churches in the city though its façade, adorned with statues of saints, was redesigned at the end of the 1500s. It contains a splendid fresco by Jacopo Bellini. The **Loggia della Gran Guardia** is an elegant 16th century monument and was once the home of Padua's High Council. It was altered by Falconetto in 1545. At the end of a long stairway the façade gives way to a ground floor portico while the first floor is broken up by an elegant mullioned window with two lights and flanked by two mullioned windows with three lights; a balustrade divides the two floors along the entire length of the Loggia. The interior hosts sixty five lacunar frescoed at the end of the 1600s by Pier Antonio Torri.

Passing through the clock arch one arrives in the Corte del Capitaniato where the **Loggia del Capitaniato** stands, believed to be the work of **Andrea Moroni**. From here one enters the *Sala dei Giganti* which is what remains of the old reign of the former rulers of Padua, the Carraresi. It's an elegant 14th century construction believed to be the work of **Domenico di Firenze**.

The splendid Cappella degli Scrovegni

Here it was where Giotto paved the way for oil painting

The most important cycle of frescoes depicting the life of Christ and Mary which were to open a new chapter in the history of western figurative art

Left: *the façade of the* Cappella degli Scrovegni.
Below: *the interior with the cycle of frescoes by* Giotto *which depict the life of* Jesus and Mary.

Tucked away in the gardens of the Arena is the small monument which contains such a huge treasure. The *Cappella degli Scrovegni* is where **Giotto**'s magnificent cycle of frescoes depicting the theme of Christian redemption through the lives of Jesus and Mary and which were executed in the early part of the 14th century. The simple chapel which was once a part of the **Palazzo Scrovegni** was built by **Enrico Scrovegni** (who was buried here) as a testament to his father. It was in the years 1304-5 that Giotto and his pupils painted the vast cycle of frescoes.

The exterior of the chapel is austere; the interior consists of one aisle. The *high altar* contains a group of sculptures, *the Virgin, Child and Angels* by **Giovanni Pisano**; Behind the altar is the *tomb of Enrico Scrovegni*. Together with the frescoes in Assisi and the later ones in Santa Croce in Florence, this cycle of frescoes constitutes a decisive innovation in the history of art, marking as they do a movement away from the flat schematic Byzantine style towards a more expressive and three dimensional perception of painting. Giotto, in fact, places his figures against backgrounds in a rich reciprocal relationship which, in many ways, was to change the spatial composition of figurative painting.

Giotto tells the story of Christ and Mary

The story of Mary and Jesus as painted by Giotto develops over thirty eight scenes arranged in three parallel sequences on the lateral walls which are painted the same color blue as the background of the frescoes. An *Annunciation* sits on the arch of the presbytery while a *Last Judgement* adorns the wall of the entrance. Low down and forming a fourth lateral sequence we find the allegories of the *Seven Deadly Sins* and the *Seven Cardinal Virtues*. Beginning at the left-hand wall we see: *the Expulsion of Joachim from the Temple, Joachim among the Shepherds, Annunciation to Anna, Sacrifice of Joachim, Vi-*

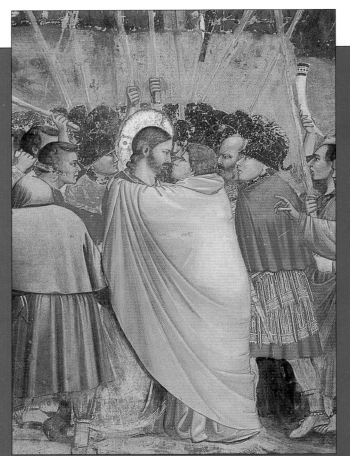

Some of Giotto's frescoes from the Scrovegni Chapel. Above, clockwise: the Judas Kiss, the Baptism of Christ. Enrico Scrovegni offers Mary the Chapel *(detail from the* Last Judgement*).* Flight into Egypt.

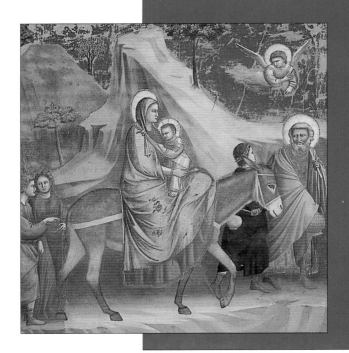

Some of Giotto's frescoes in the Scrovegni Chapel. Above, clockwise: The Last Judgement *(entrance wall of the Chapel).* The Expulsion of Joachim from the Temple. The Inferno *(detail from the* Last Judgement*).*

sion of Joachim, Meeting of Joachim and Anna.

The higher sequence on the left hand wall depicts: *Nativity, Presentation in the Temple, Presentation of the Rods to Simeon, Watching of the Rods, Marriage of the Virgin to Joseph, the Virgin's Return Home.*

Over the chancel arch we find: *God the Father Dispatching Gabriel* and, below, the *Annunciation* and, still lower, *Visitation.*

The second sequence on the right-hand wall depict: *Nativity, Adoration of the Magi, Presentation of Jesus in the Temple, Flight into Egypt, Massacre of the Innocents.*

Continuing along the left-hand wall we see: *Dispute with the Elders, Baptism of Christ, Marriage at Cana, Raising of Lazarus, Entry into Jerusalem, Expulsion from the Temple.*

The third sequence on the right-hand wall depicts: *Last Supper, Washing of the Feet, Betrayal of Christ, Christ before Caiaphas, Mocking of Christ.*

The third left-hand sequence depicts: *Way to Calvary, Crucifixion, Deposition, Angel at the Empty Tomb, Noli me tangere, Ascension, Pentecost.*

The apse of the chapel is frescoed by the so-called Maestro del coro Scrovegni, probably a pupil of Giotto's.

The Cathedral and the Baptistry

Many styles and hands, including those of
Michelangelo, went into the building
of Padua's Duomo. And the 13th century Baptistery
contains fine frescoes by Giusto de' Menabuoi

Above: the façade of Padua's Cathedral. Below: the stunning interior of the Cathedral.

At the heart of the city, on the site of an old market rises Padua's **Duomo**, dedicated to Santa Maria Assunta. It's very much a hybrid of styles as many architects and artists had a hand in its construction through the centuries.

It was built on the site of an old church which was destroyed by the Hungarians sometime before the 1000s and then rebuilt at the beginning of the 12th century. In 1547, thanks to the efforts of Bishop Francesco Pisani, it was decided to raise a new cathedral worthy of Padua. The competition to find a design was not hugely successful – the initial project drawn up by **Andrea Da Valle** was contested by Sansovino and subsequently rejected in favor of a design by Michelangelo which in turn was modified and then executed by Da Valle. One of the building's two cupolas was erected by **Squarcina**. A century later, the *Cappella della Madonna* was built followed by, at the end of the 1600s, the *Cappella del Santissimo*. The unfinished façade was begun by **Frigimelica** in 1730. The interior is arranged around a Latin-cross plan and almost all of its paintings are from the 18th century. The *Monument to the Bishop Pietro Barocci* by **Tullio Lombardo** though dates

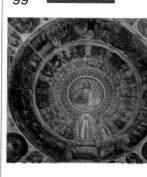

back to the 15th century. The depiction of the *Madonna with Child* in the right transept is held to have once belonged to the poet Petrarch. The cathedral has ten chapels which all contain paintings of some value. The *Sacristy* is worth investigating with its large 16th century *Armadio-Reliquario* as is the *Crypt* which is entered from the central aisle.

Alongside the Duomo we find the **Baptistry** (built in 1260 on an older version) whose interior is entirely covered by a magnificent cycle of frescoes by the Florentine painter **Giusto de' Menabuoi** in which he narrates the entire sacred story, from the Old Testament to the Life of Christ and Mary, from Genesis to Apocalypse – a vast and stunning *biblia pauperum* which perhaps has no equal in Italian art of that time.

Above, left: the façade of the **Baptistry** *and a detail from* **Paradise**, *one of* **Giusto de' Menabuoi**'s *frescoes inside.*

Delicacies of Paduan cuisine

It has already be mentioned that rice reigns supreme in the kitchens of Padua. A similar case can also be made for polenta which can be served up in the many variety of forms indicated previously in these pages in the Spotlight. Poultry is a great favorite in the area and the locals have their own special ways of preparing it as is also the case with oca in pignata *(goose). The famous chicken* al- la padovana *for example is fried with onions and butter; a beaten egg is then added and a sprinkling of lemon juice. What in Venice is famously known as* fegato alla veneziana *(liver) takes a different form in Padua and is known as* figà a la sbròdega. *As for desserts, well worth trying are the crumbly* soleti *(made from yellow flour and sultanas) and the well known* fugassa *which is a form of focaccia.*

PRATO DELLA VALLE

Padua's most original monument.
An enticing landscape of statues and bridges
created by the genius of Memmo

Giorgio Fossati: the race track in **Prato della Valle** *(mid 18th century).* **Below:** *a panoramic view of* **Prato della Valle.**

It might be said that Prato della Valle is one of the biggest and most impressive piazzas in Europe. Here, in ancient Roman times, stood the **Teatro Zairo**. Later, the area remained for centuries a pestilent marshland until, in the 18th century, it was reclaimed and used to create the piazza you see today.

This ambitious urban project, today nestling amidst a backdrop of stately palaces and containing the **Basilica di Santa Giustina,** was gotten underway in 1775 when architecture student **Andrea Memmio**, who was also the *Provveditore Straordinario* of the Republic (a kind of head supervisor or councillor by today's standards), designed this vast impressive monument and got **Domenico Cerato** to build it. An elliptical piazza was thus created which had at its center an island known as *Isola Memmia*. It is surrounded by a canal while four bridges connect the island to a circular tree-lined promenade graced with statues and obelisks. The overall effect, splendid in its time, has unfortunately been marred a little by the city traffic. The walkways are graced with obelisks and no less than seventy eight statues of the Bonazza school (one, of the

mathematician *Poleni*, was the work of the young **Canova**). The vast space, the cool white of the marble, the hypnotic lull of the waterways make of Prato della Valle one of the most spectacular urban spaces in Italy, if not the whole of Europe. Today, a modern fountain stands at the center of the island. According to some experts, the entire design might also have been created to represent a symbolic journey, perhaps linked to certain Massonic initiation rites and beliefs which Memmo himself shared.

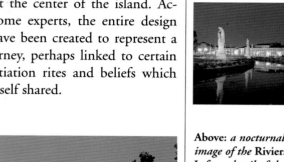

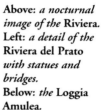

Above: *a nocturnal image of the* Riviera. Left: *a detail of the* Riviera del Prato *with statues and bridges.* Below: *the* Loggia Amulea.

Loggia Amulea: a 19th century Paduan jewel

On Prato delle Valle stands the elegant **Loggia Amulea**, a reconstruction in a neo-Gothic style of a previous building which owed its existence to Cardinal Marco Antonio Da Mula and was destroyed in a fire in the 1800s.

The Loggia, a lively mixture of black and white marble, terracotta and stone, is supported on ten pilasters and its façade was the work of **Eugenio Maestri** around 1860. It was restored in 1994.

The statues of Dante and Giotto are by **Vincenzo Vela** and have graced the Loggia since 1865.

The Amulea is a significant testament to the neo-medieval revival which was popular in Padua for a while.

The Basilica of Santa Giustina
Behind a bare and commanding façade lies one of the purest examples of Renaissance architecture

This immense basilica with its unfinished façade was raised in the 16th century by **Andrea Moroni** on the remains of a previous Christian church built on the place dedicated to the Christian martyr Giustina who was executed by the pagan Romans. There are still traces of the old church in the form of the *Sacello di San Prosdocimo* (the burial place of Padua's first bishop).

The interior of the building is vast and consists of three aisles with numerous side chapels which crowd the area behind the apse and are overhung by orientalizing small cupolas.

The Basilica is graced by some superb works of art, the most notable of which being **Paolo Veronese**'s large altarpiece of the *Martyrdom of St Justina*. Interesting too is the large 15th century *wooden cross*, sometimes positioned at the center of the central aisle.

Another work of note to be found in the Basilica is the large *Pietà* sculpted by **Parodi** in the 17th century. There's also the richly evocative Sacello di San Prosdocimo which dates back to the 5th century and contains an old marble altar with an effigy of the saint between two palms. The *choirs* are of great interest too. The *tomb of Ludovico Barbo* can be found in the **Coro Vecchio** (Old Choir).

Above: *the so-called "pozzo dei martiri" inside the* Basilica. Right: *the commanding* façade *and vast* interior *of the* Basilica di Santa Giustina.

The Basilica di Sant'Antonio
The most eminent of Padua's religious buildings, visited by believers from all over the world

Now it's time to investigate the most eminent of Padua's religious buildings, the **Basilica del Santo** which every year attracts hordes of visitors. The building has an eight-domed roof which combines a medley of Romanesque, Gothic and Byzantine influences and two octagonal campanili. The history of the basilica is a rich saga of additions, alterations and restorations. The small **Chiesetta di Santa Maria Mater Domini**, which previously occupied the site, was donated to St Anthony. When Anthony died in 1331, the influx of pilgrims was so great (he was canonized only a year after his death) that it became necessary

Left: *the* Basilica di Sant'Antonio *which dominates the city of Padua.* Inset: *the venerated* statue of Sant'Antonio.

Sant'Antonio
A thousand years of history

The Franciscan, Antonio da Lisbona, was born in Lisbon in 1195. He moved to Italy and for two years preached in Padua. He died in 1231 in the Santuario dell'Arcella, near the city. He was canonized a year later and, in his honor, the city of Padua began building a church on the site where the Romanesque church of Mater Domini had previously stood. The church has been enriched and restored many times in the course of the centuries but the cult of St Anthony remains as fervid as ever and every year thousands of pilgrims visit his tomb.

to build a larger and more worthy church on the site of the old one. In the middle of the 1200s, the nave came into being, followed soon after by the two lateral aisles, though the precise date and the names of the architects involved has remained something of a mystery. It is however known that at least twice the Basilica came close to being destroyed, once in the 1500s when it was shaken by a hurricane and once in the 1700s when a fire broke out and threatened to engulf the entire structure. In the 1800s improvements were carried out, like the three large bronze doors on the façade. The façade, on the ground level, is graced by four tall, blind arches which support a gallery endowed with no less than seventeen elegant columns and, higher still, a marble balustrade onto which the central rose window looks out. On the lunette of the *Porta Maggiore* there's a copy of a fresco by **Mantegna** which depicts *St Anthony and Bernard*.

The vast, solemn and stately interior of the Basilica, constructed in the form of the Latin cross (to an architectural design which probably originated from the other side of the Alps), contains a multitude of artistic treasures and is graced by numerous chapels and altars. The chief treasures of the Basilica are the frescoed *Transept* and the *High Altar*, adorned by masterpieces of the great **Donatello**. The High Altar has been altered many times and the present configuration, designed by **Camillo Boito** in 1895, is held to be a faithful reproduction of Donatello's original altar. Donatello was also responsible for all the magnificent sculptures: the central bronze *Crucifix* was perhaps the first work of the artist during his stay in Padua (1443-44). Seven large statues representing the *Virgin* and several saints provide a striking setting for the Crucifix. Admirable too are the large bronze panels which grace the walls and celebrate the mir-

Above: the splendidly decorated Cappella del Tesoro. *Right: the bas-reliefs of the* Cappella dell'Arca del Santo *and a view of the ex-voto near the* Altar of Sant'Antonio.

The High Altar *of the* Basilica di Sant'Antonio *with statues and* Crucifix *by* Donatello. Inset: Equestrian statue of Erasmo da Narni, *known as* "Il Gattamelata".

acles of St Anthony, including the *Miracle of the Mule and the Eucharist,* the *Miracle of the Repentant Son,* the *Miracle of the Avaricious Heart* and the *Miracle of the Talking newly-born Child.* From the Donatello school, there's also a *Deposition* and a *Pietà* which form part of the complex overall structure of the High Altar. The Transept, which forms a kind of chapel, is endowed with an extraordinary cycle of frescoes by **Altichiero Altichieri** and **Jacopo Avanzo** depicting, next to a large *Crucifixion*, scenes from the life of San Jacopo. The fresco depicting the *Privy Council* features portraits of some of Padua's notable citizens in the

The Paduan masterpieces of Donatello

A life-size Crucifix, *the equestrian statue of Gattamelata and the statues and bas-reliefs of the High Altar in the Basilica del Santo are the masterpieces which the Florentine sculptor* Donatello *bequeathed to Padua in the years around 1444, the same Padua which Giotto had enriched with his work in the Scrovegni Chapel. The Crucifix in the Basilica was the first life-size bronze cross of the Renaissance. The perfect anatomical handling, the powerful realism, the perfection of the chisel all combine to create a marvellous spiritual tension.*

As for the Gattamelata, in the piazza of the Basilica del Santo, it is a monument to Erasmo da Narni, known as Gattamelata, a powerful warrior and head of the victorious Venetian army. It was the first large equestrian monument of the Renaissance, based on Roman statue, especially that of the emperor Marcus Aurelius. However, Donatello's horse

is bigger and more powerful and Gattamelata's armor including a Medusa head at the center, is quintessentially a product of the15th century.

The statues and reliefs by Donatello which grace the High Altar of the Basilica are also masterpieces of their kind and include a statue of the Enthroned Madonna with Child, *statues of the six patron saints of Padua,* St Louis, St Francis, St Daniel, St Anthony, St Justina *and* St Prosdocimus. *There are then the stunning reliefs of the* Four Miracles of St Anthony *above the predella.*

Madonna Mora

One of the Basilica's chapels, next to the *Cappella del Tesoro*, takes the name of the *Cappella della Madonna Mora* from the statue which is preserved within its walls and which has created a cult that the Paduans take very seriously. The statue dates back to the 14th century and was the work of **Rinaldino di Francia**. It depicts the *Virgin standing with the Child in her arms* and both figures wear crowns. The Madonna wears a red robe and an embroidered blue cloak; her face is dark-skinned - hence the name of the *Black Madonna*.

1300s, including the poet Petrarch. A place of special worship is the stately *Cappella del Tesoro* which contains the reliquaries of St Anthony. The remains of the Saint were in fact brought here in 1745. The Chapel was built to a circular plan by **Filippo Parodi** at the end of the 1600s who also executed the statues in the style of Bernini which adorn the Chapel. Beneath three large arches on the far wall lay the reliquaries, including the tongue of St Anthony and the crystal cross.

The other chapels too, built by representatives of various nations who were studying in Padua at the celebrated university, contain many fine works of art – there's the *Cappella della Nazione Germanica*, the *Cappella di Santo Stefano*, the *Cappella di San Stanislao*, of Polish origin and the *Cappella del beato Luca*, built in the 14th century but only recently dedicated to the friend of St Anthony, Luca Belludi whose remains are preserved here. This chapel is particularly important because it contains no less than sixty-eight frescoes depicting scenes from the *lives of San Filippo* and *San Giacomo* by the 14th century Florentine painter **Giusto de' Menabuoi**. The central *Enthroned Madonna with Child* is especially beautiful. Another center of devout worship attracting pilgrims from all over the country is the *Cappella del Santo* which, since 1310, has contained the *tomb of St Anthony*. This lays behind a green marble arch adorned with many votive offerings and is reached by way of a small staircase behind five arches supported by elegant columns. Five arches grace the far

wall of the chapel with nine large reliefs in marble depicting stories of St Anthony by various artists from different periods of history. **Jacopo Sansovino** was responsible for some of the *Miracles of the Saint* while other 16th century reliefs were the work of **Tullio** and **Antonio Lombardo**.

Other important works of art in the Basilica include the sepulchral monuments like the *tomb of Pietro Bembo* (1547) with its so-called *Madonna del Pilastro* which is placed on and supported by a huge 15th century marble pillar and was the work of **Jacopo da Montagnana**. Finally, anyone visiting the Basilica cannot leave without setting foot in the four *Cloisters* and the *Sacristy*.

Above, left: Cappella di Sant'Antonio; right: *frescoes by* Giusto de' Menabuoi *in the* Cappella del Beato Luca *in the* Basilica del Santo. Below: *a view of the* Noviziato cloisters *by the* Basilica.

The Oratory of San Giorgio and the Scuola del Santo

A vast cycle of frescoes by Altichiero in the Oratory and some masterpieces by the young Titian in the Scuola

This oratory was once the chapel of the noble Lupi di Soragno family and dates back to 1384.

In its bare plan it is quite reminiscent of the Scrovegni Chapel.

The interior is entirely covered in frescoes by the 14th century Veronese artist **Altichiero Alticheri**. The huge cycle consists of twenty two scenes which occupy the ceiling as well as the walls and narrate the life of Jesus together with stories of saints including Catherine, Lucy and George.
The work as a whole is a lively composition of fine portraiture, playful anecdote and vibrant color.

The **Scuola del Santo** was

erected immediately after the death of Sant'Antonio. It became a small church in 1427, was enlarged at the beginning of the 1500s and altered two centuries later with especial attention paid to the façade.

Today it's importance derives from the fact that it contains an important cycle of paintings from the early 1500s dedicated to the life of Sant'Antonio among which are some early works by the young **Titian**.

Attributed to him are the episodes of the *Miracle of the New Born Child*, the *Miracle of the Irascible Son* and the *Miracle of the Healed Foot*.

Above: *the* façade *of the* Scuola del Santo. Below, left: Saint Anthony coaxing a new-born child into speech, *by* Titian *in the* Scuola del Santo. Below: St Giorgio baptizes King Sevio *(detail), by* Altichiero *in the* Oratory of San Giorgio.

The Church of the Eremitani and the Museo Civico

In the old monastery complex stands this 13th century church, next to the museum, with splendid frescoes by Mantegna

Above: *the façade of the* church of the Eremitani. Below: *a detail of the tomb of Federico Guglielmo d'Orange.* Right: *the interior of the church.*

The **church of the Eremitani**, on the south side of the park near the Cappella dei Scrovegni, was built in 1276 and then, in the following centuries, the side chapels were added. The upper section of the façade is made of brick; the lower part of the façade has a broad doorway flanked on either side by four marble arches which in turn rest upon four sepulture arches, a model later employed by Leon Battista Alberti for the Tempio Malatestiano in Rimini.

On the southern side of the church there's a beautiful 15th century doorway surmounted by an edicola with carvings depicting the *Months* by **Niccolò Baroncelli** which, unfortunately, are in a bad state of decay.

The interior of the church, a single broad aisle with a wooden ship's-keel roof, is stately. Two *tombs* by the Venetian **Andriolo de Santi** stand out, that of *Jacopo da Carrara* (1350) and *Ubertino da Carrara* (1345). In the north aisle is the *tomb of Marco Mantova-Benavides*, a 16th century work with statues by the Flo-

rentine **Bartolomeo Ammannati**.

Once the pride and joy of the church were the frescoes in the *Cappella Ovetari* by **Mantegna** and **Vivarini** which unfortunately suffered huge damage during the Second World War and only fragments now remain.

Padua's **Museo Civico** now occupies the old **Convent of the Eremitani** and incorporates a fascinating archaeological section and an important art gallery as well as a numismatics section known as the **Collezione Bottacin**.

The archaeological section contains a fine collection of paeleo-Venetic artefacts (among the tombs, there's the beautiful *Tomba dei vasi borchiati)*, many treasures from Etruscan times including bronzes and many exhibits from Roman antiquity (the beautiful head of Aphrodite, a splendid portrait of Augustus and a bust of Silenus). There are also early Christian antiquities. The archaeological section of the museum concludes with the 13th century *Cappellina* which contains examples of Pre-christian art.

But the real treasure house of the museum is provided by the **Pinacoteca**. This art gallery contains works by **Giotto** (the *Arena Chapel Crucifix*), **Squarcione** (*polyptych*), **Jacopo Bellini** (*Christ in Limbo*), **Giovanni Bellini** (*Portrait of a Young Senator*), **Giorgione** (*Leda and the Swan and Country Idyll*), **Paolo Veronese** (*The Last Supper, Martyrdom of S. Justina*) and **Jacopo Tintoretto** (*Supper in the House of Simon*). This very impressive collection of paintings also includes fine works by **Bassano**, **Piazzetta**, **Tiepolo** and **Longhi**.

Clockwise: Giotto's Crucifix, *once in the* Cappella degli Scrovegni; Leda and the Swan, *attributed to* Giorgione; Portrait of a Young Senator *by* Giovanni Bellini; Country Idyll *attribuited to* Giorgione.

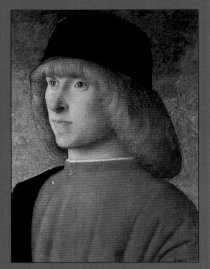

What was once an elegant theater

Loggia and Odeo Cornaro

Loggia and Odeo Cornaro, an evocative corner of Padua.

At the beginning of the 1500s a Venetian humanist by the name of Alvise Cornaro had the idea of adding first a loggia and then an odeo to his palace in order to host theater productions and especially the work of his contemporary Ruzante. The task was entrusted to and executed by **Giovan Maria Falconetto** and thus the elegant **Loggia** and **Odeo** began functioning as a theatrical environment. The loggia has two storeys and is graced by five arches with Doric columns and, above, by two windows and three niches with statues. The Odeo, on the other hand, has a niche and two edicolas on the ground floor and three windows above. This corner of Padua thus preserves something of the great Humanist tradition.

Rice and risotto with flair

Rice is the great mainstay of Paduan cuisine. The famous Venetian risi and bisi *also enjoys great popularity in Padua but there are other rice-based dishes well worth trying like* risi e bruscandoli *(rice with the tops of hops), or rice cooked with celery and tomatoes. There's also a variation of risi e bisi with strips of goose cooked in its own fat, or* risotto con i rovinassi *(chicken giblets). Other rice dishes include* risotto with zucca *(pumpkin),* risotto con le ciche *(chicken kidneys),* risotto con le quaglie *(quail),* risotto con le rane *(frogs) and* risotto e luganega *(the local sausages). In short, anyone visiting the city who wishes to enter into its culture and spirit should not leave without sampling at least one of the many rice-based dishes for which Padua is renowned.*

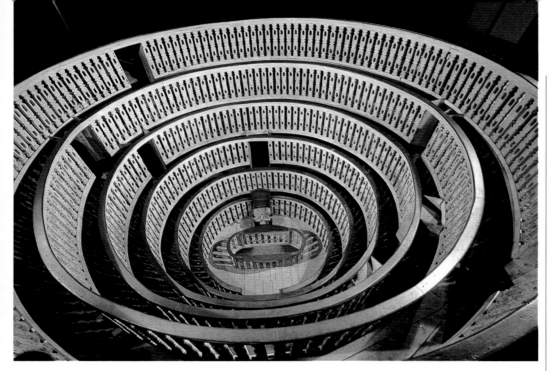

The stately
Anatomical Theater
of the **University**.

Palazzo del Bo, where Galileo taught

Eight glorious centuries of learning

The **University of Padua**, founded as long ago as 1222, is one of the oldest and most famous in Europe. Two centuries later, in 1493, it was established on the present site where previously an inn had stood called *Il Bo* (The Ox) from which the University derives its nick-name. Beside the general architectural elegance of the building, points of interest include the large elliptical **Anatomical Theater**, built in 1594, the first in Europe, by **Girolamo Fabrizio d'Acquapendente** and the *Cattedra* where **Galileo** is believed to have taught dur-

Below, left: *the teaching desk of* Galileo Galilei, statue of Elena Lucrezia Cornaro Priscopia, *the world's first female graduate;* Palinuro, *sculpture by* Arturo Martini *(Hall of the Heroes).*

Portrait of Galileo Galilei. **Right: the Aula Magna of Padua's old university. Inset:** *the* **Caffè Pedrocchi,** *one of Italy's most famous cafés.*

ing his time in Padua.

The University's *Cortile Antico* is a courtyard with a double order of loggias designed by **Andrea Moroni** in the 16th century; the façade is attributed to **Vincenzo Scamozzi**. Works by various 20th century artists, sculptures by **Arturo Martini** and **Giacomo Manzù** and paintings by **Filippo De Pisis** and **Gino Severini** adorn the various halls and stairways while the splendid *Aula Magna* was restored by the great Italian architect **Giò Ponti** in 1942. Other curiosities include the portraits of Venetian dukes in the *Sala del senato accademico* and the statue of the first female ever to be given a degree in Europe, Elena Lucrezia Cornaro Piscopia.

200 years
Caffè Pedrocchi

It's one of the most celebrated historical cafés in the whole of Italy and for more than a century has provided an habitual meeting place for students and professors of the University. It was also the hub of the patriotic rebellion against the Austrians in 1848. The Café was built in 1831 for Antonio Pedrocchi by the architect Giuseppe Jappelli *on the remains of an old pagan temple. In 1883* the same architect added the part known as **Pedrocchino**. *The café gradually took on its character which is now distinguished by its different colored rooms. There's a green room with an open fire, a red room with columns, a white room and then the Moorish room, the Greek room, the Roman room, the Renaissance room, the Baroque room and the Rossini room, named after the composer Gioacchino Rossini. Today the caffè Pedrocchi is called the café without doors because of its custom of opening until very late and because it preserves the spirit of free and lively discussion.*

From the Brenta Riviera to the Euganean Hills

The great villas of the Padua region

In the environs of Padua, along the stretch of land known as the Riviera del Brenta after the river which runs through it, there are a great number of splendid villas, as is the case throughout the Veneto. To reach this area by car from Padua one should leave the city by Pontile Bassanello and take the road known as the Burchiello which leads to the Riviera.

In Stra there's the splendid 18th century **Villa Pisani** which besides containing frescoes painted by Giovan Battista Tiepolo also possesses a large park.

Another magnificent building is **Villa Bon** and, nearby, **Palazzo Ferretti-Mocenigo**, built by **Vincenzo Scamozzi**. Crossing the countryside almost to the point of reaching the lagoon of Venice one encounters the famous villa known as "La Malcontenta", designed by **Andrea Palladio**. The other villas in the environs of Padua worthy of attention include **Villa Barbarigo** and **Villa Velluti**.

Clockwise: *the 18th century* Villa Pisani *in Stra, with frescoes by Tiepolo;* Villa "La Malcontenta" *by* Andrea Palladio; Villa Barbarigo; Villa Velluti.

The Euganean hills
Splendid hills, historical towns, spas and good food

Three views of the Euganean hills, abounding in historical towns and spas.

The **Euganean hills**, in the southern part of Veneto near Padua, constitute the chief hilly region of the Padana plains and offer a secluded and fertile oasis of natural beauty. The profile of the volcanic formation of the hills is represented by impressive conical reliefs towering over an area of more than three hundred square kilometers.

The highest peak is **Monte Venda** which rises up to a height of 603 meters. The area owes a great deal of its fame and popularity to the wealth of its springs and spas, since the waters falling from the foothills of the Alps gathers in underground pools and then, seeping back up to the surface, acquires precious salt traces from the rocks. The health-giving properties of these waters are today internationally renowned though as far back as two thousand years ago the Romans had turned the Abano area into a popular spa. The Euganean hills offer landscapes of breathtaking beauty, but as well as providing rare natural resources, they also contain things of artistic and his-

torical interest. Vineyards and woods animate landscapes which are enriched by Roman archaeological sites as well as medieval and Renaissance constructions and remains – thus, villas, castles, sanctuaries and abbeys are scattered throughout the region.

A nature reserve has recently been created inside the territory of the Euganean hills comprising of an area of 18,000 hectares – a sign of how important this environment is held to be. A lavish variety of flora adorns the hills so that you'll come across broom and olives as well as birch, beech and fir trees. In recent times the Euganean hills have become an immense tourist attraction and not only because of the spas. In fact, the local people are renowned for their hospitality and generosity. Well worth seeing are the old towns of Este, Monselice and Arquà Petrarca where the poet Petrarch spent the last years of his life and where his house has been turned into a museum for the Italian writer. And then of course there's Abano, famous for its health spas.

Abano Terme

Elegant town with famous spas dating back to Roman times

Abano Terme is a small, pretty town with a neoclassical look about it with its wide tree-lined avenues, tidy piazzas, a large park and numerous spas. The hotels themselves are elegant buildings, in particular, the neoclassical *Royal Orologio* designed in 1825 by **Giuseppe Jappelli**. The hot springs of Abano were celebrated as far back as in the Roman times when they were held to be sacred waters. In the 6th century, Theodorius revived them and in the 13th century they were taken under protection by the city council of Padua. Today they attract visitors from all over Europe. The springs themselves contain sodium chloride, bromide, iodine and lithium which gush forth at a temperature of 87 degrees and are used for mud baths. But even those who do not come for the hot springs can enjoy the peaceful charm of this small elegant town in the heart of the Euganean hills. The Palladian-inspired **Villa Malipiero** and, in Piazza San Lorenzo, the **Cathedral** and its 14th century *Campanile*.

The old Santuario of Monteortone. Above: *the* Duomo of Abano Terme *with the 14th century* Campanile.

Other spas and an old sanctuary

The visitor to Abano should also stop off at the impressive old Santuario di Santa Maria di Monteortone. *Built, it would appear, by* Pietro *and* Tullio Lombardo, *it's a 15th century temple no more than a kilometer and a half from Abano and is the place where an image appeared that was venerated as the Madonna. Inside there are frescoes depicting the story of Mary and painted by a pupil of Mantegna's. Not far from Abano, constituting a unique network of spas, we arrive in the the locality of Montegrotto Terme where impressive archaeological sites can be admired, containing the remains of Roman bath houses and equipped with a plumbing system, large tubs and even a small theater of which the cavea is still visible. The Romans considered these springs sacred and invested great faith in the healing properties of these waters.*

Arquà Petrarca

A charming historical town which cherishes the memory of the poet who lived here at the end of the 1300s

The poet Francesco Petrarca. Above: the house where Petrarca was born in Arquà.

Arquà is pervaded by and dedicated to the memory of the great poet Francesco Petrarca who chose to spend the last years of his life here (1370-1374). His tomb, a red marble arch, can be found in Piazza Roma. There are many splendid buildings in the town and its surroundings, including **Palazzo Contarini-Beolco** which belonged to the family of the great dramatist from Padua Ruzante, the **Loggia dei Vicari** and the **Oratorio della Trinità** (1181) where there's a *Santissima Trinità* by **Palma il Giovane**. But the pride and joy of Arquà is without question the **House of Petrarch**, built for him and then enriched with frescoes two centuries later. Here Petrarch lived with his daughter Francesca and truly poignant are the small rooms which have since been decorated with pictures inspired by his poetry. There's also the study and chair where Petrarch studied and many illustrious poets have passed through the house in homage to the Italian writer including Byron and Carducci.

Risotto, mushrooms and fine wines

Eating in these parts is a treat since, besides the excellent food, the region also offers top quality wines. The grapes that grow in the Euganean hills are tended with great expertise and of a very high quality. Among the most renowned wines of the region you might try a Colli Euganei *white, a* Cabernet, *a* Chardonnay *or a* Pinot bianco. *In Arquà, home of the poet Petrarch, wines worth trying include the* Rosso dei Colli Euganei, Merlot, Gemola *and an excellent* Cabernet. *Three spumanti also stand out – the* Rosso del Venda, *the* Serprina *and the* Moscato di Arquà.
As for food, it's Paduan cuisine which dominates (see the Padua inset). Among the most popular local dishes we find risotto ai funghi *(rice with mushrooms),* torresani allo spiedo *(pigeon on the spit) and excellent game. The mushrooms are superb and always available in these parts. In the Este region, white truffles are very popular. And to help digest your meal, what better than a glass of Veneto grappa?*

Este
Ancient, dignified and famous for its archaeological museum

Situated on the Bisatto canal thirty kilometers from Padua, this elegant and historic town has ancient origins and was the center of pre-Roman culture in the Veneto seven centuries before Christ. The **Museo Nazionale Atestino** contains various treasures from this period. Among the wide collection of rare artefacts displayed on its premises, of particular interest are the vase decorated in the form of a palmiped, the famous *Situla Benvenuti*, carved with a burin and chisel and depicting battle and ceremonial scenes and the noteworthy bronze statue known as the *Dea di Caldevigo*. From a later period is the *Medaglione aureo di Augusto*. And don't leave the museum without seeing the 16th century panel of *Madonna with Child* by **Cima da Conegliano**.

But there's more to Este. Apart from offering enchanting excursions into the nearby Euganean hills, Este is also endowed with a number of impressive historic buildings. There's the **Chiesa di San Martino**, the oldest church in the town, the 18th century Domenican **Basilica di Santa Maria delle Grazie**, the 16th century **Chiesa di Santa Maria delle Consolazioni** and the 17th century **Tempio della Beata Vergine della Salute**. Finally, there's the 18th century **Duomo**, dedicated to Santa Tecla which contains a masterpiece by **Giambattista Tiepolo** in its apse: *Santa Tecla Freeing Este from the Plague*.

Monselice
A castle, a wealth of history and splendid Palladian villas

Today an important industrial center, but once enclosed within five city walls, Monselice has much to offer in the way of historical treasures. On top of the hill stands the fortress, **la Rocca** and its keep which the Holy Roman Emperor Frederick II had built and which was later destroyed and rebuilt. Within the city itself there's the **Castello** which is actually a complex of buildings and was once the heavily-defended dwelling of Ezzelino da Romano, the lord of this territory; today, it is utilized as a museum. The palace is well furnished and among its curiosities contains a towering fireplace with small majolica columns. There is also a collection of weapons, ceramics, sculptures and paintings. Having visited the **Duomo di Santa Giustina**, perhaps the chief attractions of Monselice are two splendid villas: **Villa Pisani**, a 16th century masterpiece by **Andrea Palladio** and beautifully frescoed inside; and **Villa Nani Mocenigo**, also built in the 16th century though later enlarged, with its bewitching terraced staircase adorned with statues and an impressive nymphaeum.

Piazzale della Rotonda offers a splendid sweeping view of the surrounding countryside and, before leaving Monselice, a visit to the **Santuario delle Sette Chiese** is recommended, a sacred avenue containing six chapels, concluding with the domed and arcaded **Chiesa di San Giorgio**.

The **Duomo Vecchio** *of Monselice.* **Above, from left to right:** *the* **Castle at Este**, *a view of the town of* **Monselice** *and the* **Castle.**

A blend of natural beauty and artistic masterpieces
The splendors of the province of Vicenza

The vicentina countryside. Above, left to right: aerial view of Vicenza's historical center; an unusual panorama of the city. Below, right: Palladio's "Basilica".

The province of Vicenza is blessed with a wealth of beautiful landscapes, important art treasures, small towns seeped in history and a fine reputation for its traditional cuisine. Vicenza lies in the Veneto pianura, among lush hills and is surrounded by mountains.

Among the most significant places of the region it's worth listing Bassano del Grappa, Marostica, Thiene, at the foot of the mountains, the busy woollen manufacturing towns of Schio and Valdagno and then, Arzignano, Montecchio Maggiore and Lonigo.

Also worth mentioning are the internationally renowned spa center at Recoaro and the tablelands of Tonezza and Asiago, both popular winter resorts for tourists.

A feature of the area are the splendid villas scattered throughout the countryside — stately country or village dwellings which contain artistic treasures signed by the likes of Scamozzi, Longhena, Pizzocaro and Giambattista and Giandomenico Tiepolo.

VICENZA

Vicenza itself, small (it has a 120,000 inhabitants), prosperous, friendly and stacked with art treasures, bears the mark everywhere of its favorite son, the great architect **Andrea Palladio** whose masterpieces — from the stupendous **Basilica** in Piazza dei Signori to to the majestic **teatro Olimpico** and the many stunning palaces that line the roads — proliferate throughout the town. However, this predominion of one artist and his distinctive style does not prevent Vicenza from presenting a rich variety of styles which pay testament to its long illustrious past. This rich city was

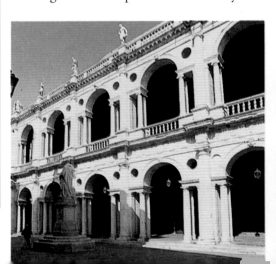

Piazza dei Signori, *heart of the city.* Below: *a fresco by* Tiepolo *in the* Villa Loschi Zileri Dal Verme.

The Roman Cryptoporticus

The criptoportico of Roman origin is actually nothing but an underground connecting passageway between two parts of a building. It has a U shape and can be found beneath **Palazzetto Proti** and the building of the new **Canonica** on the south side of Piazza del Duomo.

The cryptoporticus, which can still be traversed, consists of two lateral wings twenty seven meters long; the walls are faintly plastered and endowed with a series of embrasure windows. The flooring, once consisting of three different materials, has now almost vanished completely. The stairway leading down to the cryptoporticus has an opening which is decorated in red plaster. It's strange that this cryptoporticus appears to be at a distance from Piazza dei Signori where the old Roman forum stood. Probably it was an underground tunnel belonging to some stately building of old Vicenza.

Rich in art, prosperous and charming

The domain of Palladio, a rich variety of styles

once a Roman *Municipium.* Later it enjoyed a period of independence before succumbing to the rule of the feared Ezzelino and then the Scaligeri and Visconti families. In the 1400s it became part of the powerful Venetian Republic and was to remain under Venice's rule for centuries until the 19th century when it fell briefly to the French and then, for a longer period, to the Austrians. Therefore, strolling through the compact, elegant historic center of Vicenza, a flurry of different styles compete for attention – from the old Roman origins of the city through its predominant serene Renaissance aspects with here and there examples of Baroque and neoclassical architecture. And if Vicenza's churches all bear the stamp of diverse artistic styles, the same can be said of the city's many beautiful palaces which together perhaps constitute the jewel in its crown.

Standing in the midst of gently undulating countryside not far from the slopes of the Berici mountains at the confluence of two rivers, the Retrone and the younger Bacchiglione, Vicenza is today not only a city

with a splendid artistic heritage but also a thriving industrial center. It's one of the world's centers for gold craftsmanship as well as possessing flourishing marble, stone and ceramics industries (international fairs and shows are held every year in all these fields). Artistic activity is also widespread in the city and the drama season at the stunning Olimpico always attracts huge crowds. Finally, Vicenza offers its visitors the fruits of its traditional cuisine which, though sharing many things in common with other parts of Veneto, still retains its own personal touches.

Olimpico
The four centuries of a theater

Created by Palladio at the end of the 1500s and completed by Scamozzi, it has witnessed the staging of thousands of plays and its fixed backdrop depicts an admirable series of perspectives alluding to the ancient city of Thebes but which resemble streets of Vicenza itself

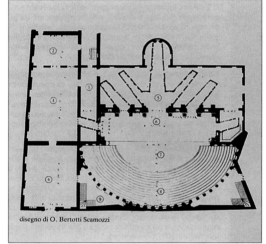

disegno di O. Bertotti Scamozzi

A view of the gardens of the Teatro Olimpico *in Vicenza designed by* Palladio. Right: *the plan of the theater in a drawing by* O. Bertotti Scamozzi.

It was the nobles of the **Accademia Olimpica** who at the end of the 1500s commissioned this beautiful theater which was to stage representations of ancient tragedy. It was designed by the great architect **Andrea Palladio** who built it in the *cortile d'armi* through which it is still reached today. Conceived in 1580, it was Palladio's last work and he died before completing it; thus it was his disciple, **Vincenzo Scamozzi**, who, in the years 1581-85, saw to the theater's completion. It was opened in 1585 with a production of Sophocles' Theban Plays. The architectural design of the theater was very much inspired by old Greek and Roman models and the principle materials used were wood, plaster and stucco, painted in such a way as to resemble marble. All the moveable props on the other hand were made of bricks.

The stage is a splendid creation, dominated by an immense and elegant *Arco di Trionfo* –adorned with a triple row of columns and pilasters that reveal a painted perspective of roads which create a strange spatial illusion of depth and substance. These are the seven streets of ancient Thebes though, in part, they resemble certain streets of Vicenza itself. The *cavea*, where the audience sits due to the lack of space, was constructed not on a semi-circular plan but is semi-elliptical and consists of thirteen tiers.

Of all the great Palladian buildings, the Olimpico represents the magnificent culmination of the architect's career. It was the last building he designed and, in many ways, the most lively and practical seeing as it still functions perfectly as a theater and has done ever since the end of the 1500s.

The old portal in the garden, the frescoes of the Odeon, the wonders of the painted backdrops, the ingenious curve of the Cavea, the statues: all creating a unique cohesion of elegance

● *The theater is reached from the courtyard of the castle, through a stone portal designed by Ottavio Bruto Revese and a beautiful garden.*

● The **Odeon**, or music hall, and the **Antiodeon** are both lavishly frescoed. The Odeon is the work of **Scamozzi** and the frescoes were executed in the 17th century by **Francesco Maffei**.

● *If the stage is impressive, no less so is the Cavea, the tiers which seat the audience. This too was the work of Palladio and is constructed according to a semi-elliptical curve in order to maximize the limited space available.*

● The **stage** where the performances unfurl is perhaps the most inventive creation of the entire theater with its central arch. The stage as a whole comprises of a façade with two rows of columns and pilasters, each of which is adorned with a niche containing a plaster statue. The perspective of the seven streets of Thebes is painted with such skill as to create an almost life-like spatial illusion.

● *Thanks to this theater which reserves its stage almost entirely for productions of ancient and classical works and Verona's Arena which essentially hosts operas (not to mention the historic Fenice theater in Venice), Veneto has every reason to feel proud of its theater.*

Above: *the* Piazzetta Palladio *in Vicenza.* Other photos on this page: *some views of the interior of the* Teatro Olimpico *designed by* Andrea Palladio.

Piazza dei Signori
heart of the city

From the splendor of the Palazzo della Ragione to the elegance of the Loggia del Capitaniato, from the slender Torre di piazza to the majestic Palazzo del Monte

Palazzo della Ragione, also known as the Basilica, Palladio's first masterpiece in Vicenza.

The true civic heart of Vicenza is **Piazza dei Signori**. Two slender elegant columns, one dedicated to Christ and constructed in the 17th century, the other surmounted by the Lion of St Mark dating back to the 15th century, stand guard in the square which is dominated by the majestic **Palazzo della Ragione** or **Basilica**, the first of **Palladio**'s masterpieces in Vicenza and another of Palladio's creations, the splendid **Loggia del Capitaniato** with its slender and stately tower, the **Torre di piazza**, also known as the Torre dei Bissari, an ancient family from the area. The brick tower extends to a height of 82 meters and was erected during the 12th century. Next to the Loggia stands the historic caffè Garibaldi. Dominating another side of the piazza is the very long

Palazzo del Monte di Pietà which incorporates the **Loggia** of the **Chiesa di San Vicenzo**, built at the beginning of the 1600s and crowned with statues. The first wing of the palazzo was built at the end of the 1400s as one of the first Italian Monte di Pietàs while the second wing, which is identical, was constructed in 1550.

The white stone Basilica with its copper ship's-keep vault adorned with a balustrade featuring statues of the ancient gods, is the true symbol of Vicenza. In truth, this palace was the fruit of a reconstruction carried out by Palladio who added a double order of loggias to the pre-existing 15th century construction and also provided an enclosed space to house a market. The splendor of the Basilica is dependant on certain recurring stylistic motifs, like the series of ogive windows along the entire length of the building's façade which open onto the loggias.

Other highly decorative touches of this building include the gargoyles and arches of the 15th century staircase and the huge *Sala del Consiglio* which is more than 25 meters high. On the ground floor traces can still be seen of the 15th century goldsmiths workshops on which the palazzo was built.

The elegant Loggia del Capitaniato was begun by Palladio in 1571. It comprises of three arches supported by immense brick columns. The rich decoration on the stucco, the balustrades and the cornices of the arches provide a light contrast to the severity of the structure. The main room of the Loggia is beautiful, flaunting as it does a rich ceiling and paintings on its walls. Next to Piazza dei Signori stands **Piazza delle Erbe**, facing which is the other side of Palladio's Basilica. This is the market piazza, dominated by the so-called **Torre del Tormento** which earned its grim name from the fact that from the 1200s it was used as a torture chamber. The *monument to Andrea Palladio* stands between the two piazzas and is often obscured by the lively stalls of the market.

Leaving the piazza two more of Vicenza's monuments are worth a look before visiting the other churches and palaces: **casa Pigafetta** and **ponte San Michele** where the two rivers, the Retrone and the Bacchiglione, meet. Casa Pigafetta was built in 1481 by **Stefano da Ravenna** and was the home of the great navigator.

It's a unique building of its kind in Veneto because it blends the ornate late-Gothic style with the blossoming spirit of the Renaissance. It's façade is impressive with its three elegant single-light windows and three balconies separated by spiral columns. As for the San Michele bridge, it was erected at the beginning of the 1600s, the work of the same constructors who had built the Rialto in Venice which it resembles in so much as it possesses only one arch and is made of semi-precious stone.

The **Loggia del Capitaniato**, *another of Palladio's masterpieces in Vicenza.*
Below: *the* **ponte San Michele**, *where the two rivers, the Retrone and the Bacchiglione meet.*

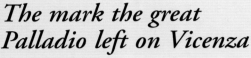

Spotlight on a master

The mark the great Palladio left on Vicenza

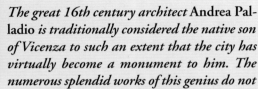

The great 16th century architect **Andrea Palladio** *is traditionally considered the native son of Vicenza to such an extent that the city has virtually become a monument to him. The numerous splendid works of this genius do not limit themselves to one style but virtually create a civilization of their own. The definitive undisputed masterpiece of Palladio is the* **Teatro Olimpico** *(Piazza Matteotti), his last work which he begun in 1580 and was completed, after his death, by Scamozzi.*

In the same piazza rises the Palladian **Palazzo Chiericati,** *which is now the Civic Museum. Also by Palladio are the* **Palazzo Porto Festa,** *one of his creations while still a young man which contains frescoes by Giam Battista Tiepolo, the* **Palazzo Barbaram da Porto** *and* **Palazzo Thiene.**

Among the great loggias by Palladio, we find the the marble **Logge della Basilica** *in Piazza dei Signori, the only one of Palladio's works in semi-precious stone, and the* **Loggia del Capitaniato** *in the same piazza which remained unfinished.*

Among the rare religious works carried out by Palladio there's the lateral doorway of the **Cathedral.** *Another of his masterpieces,* Palazzo Valmarana *can be found in Corso Fogazzaro, still another in Corso Palladio,* **Palazzo Bonin Longare** *which Scamozzi had a hand in designing, and then there's* **Palazzo Porto Breganze** *in Piazza Castello which, though designed by Palladio, was executed by Scamozzi.*

A young work of Palladio is the **Palazzo Civena Trisino.** *Finally, there's another of his major triumphs, the* **Villa Capra-Valmarana** *known as the* **Rotonda.** *Perhaps the most celebrated of all his villas, it was begun in 1550 and a full description of its charms can be found on the following pages.*

City of regal dwellings

The Palaces, masterpieces in stone

Veneto architecture leaves its mark not so much on the religious buildings, though numerous and of importance, as on the noble city palaces and country villas, all of which were built in the golden centuries of the Venetian Republic (and also during its decline in the 18th century) by the nobility of the area who divided their time between the social whirl of the city and the peaceful farming activities of the country. Side by side with Gothic buildings we thus find those later palaces which Palladio and his immediate successors created with such flair and which adorn so richly the streets of Vicenza, beginning with the stupendous **Basilica**.

Corso Palladio and Contrà Porti are perhaps the two streets in Vicenza most lavishly endowed with celebrated palaces. However there are many other examples of note in the surrounding streets, including **Palazzo Valmarana-Braga** in Corso Fogazzaro, begun by Palladio in 1556, or **Palazzo Cordellina** in Contrà Riale. The former is supported by gigantic pilasters which line the façade

and, in the courtyard, endowed with two facing loggias. The latter, typical of the neo-classical style and the work of **Ottone Calderari**, was restored after being damaged during the Second World War when frescoes hanging in some of its rooms were destroyed. In Piazza

Facing page: Casa Cogollo *known as the* Palladio. Insert, above: Palazzo Barbaran *and* Palazzo Valmarana-Braga.

San Lorenzo stands the 18th century **Palazzo Repeta-Sale** designed by Francesco Muttoni which has recently been restored.

On the threshold of Corso Palladio which is Vicenza's main street stands **Palazzo Porto Breganze**, attributed to **Palladio** but erected by his disciple **Scamozzi**. There follows the majesty of **Palazzo Bonin Longare**, Palladian in style and endowed with a spacious atrium and a large elegant reception hall connected to a loggia. Other important buildings follow including **Palazzo Bissari** with its 17th century façade and, nearby, **Palazzo Loschi Zileri del Verne**, a late 18th century construction and perhaps the masterpiece of **Ottone Calderari**.

Still on Corso Palladio, we find the stately and imposing **Palazzo Trissino**, built at the end of the 16th century for the nobleman, Galeazzo Trissino by **Vincenzo Scamozzi** and later completed and enlarged with Baroque and neo-classical touches by **Ottone Calderari**. Damaged by a fire in 1945 which reduced to ashes a number of paintings by Dorigny, it has recently been restored and is now the headquarters of the Vicenza council.

Just past Via San Gaetano, still in Corso Palladio, rises one of Vicenza's most beautiful and impressive palaces, the Gothic **Palazzo da Schio** which is also known as the **Ca' d'oro**. It was built between the 14th and 15th centuries and is a superlative example of Venetian Gothic architecture with its two orders of small balconies on the façade and its elegant mullioned windows. The Renaissance doorway is attributed to Lorenzo da Bologna.

Corso Palladio, *heart of the city.*
Below: *the entrance and the* Sala degli Stucchi *of* Palazzo Trissino.

Excellent wines in the province of Vicenza

The hills around Vicenza are strewn with well-tended vineyards which provide the grapes used to produce some of the best known wines in Italy. For example, there's the **Recioto** from Gamberella, the **Amarone** from Valpolicella, the local **Pinot grigio** and the **Pinot bianco**. The Colli Berici **Merlot** and **Cabernet** are both fine red wines as is the **Merlot Campo del Lago**. Finally, the **Braganza bianco**, the **Malvasia Capo dei fiori** and the **Prosecco** produced in the Bassano del Grappa zone are all well worth trying.

Now we move onto Contrà Porti where **Palazzo Thiene** is to be found. The façade of this splendid palace rises on a foundation of ashlar and pilasters, reputed to be the work of Lorenzo da Bologna and built at the end of the 1400s. The doorway is the work of Tommaso da Milano. The nearby **Palazzo Barbaran Porto** is another of Palladio's creations and is now the office of the Ministry of Environmental Health. Other historical buildings in this street include the Palladian **Palazzo Iseppo da Porto**, built in the middle of the 1500s and adorned with beautiful first-floor windows; the splendid **Palazzo Porto Colleoni**, another fine example of Venetian Gothic architecture with large

A typical Veneto trattoria. Above: *the 15th century* Palazzo Thiene *designed by* Lorenzo da Bologna.

The best in cuisine in Vicenza

Risi e bisi, baccalà, polenta and game

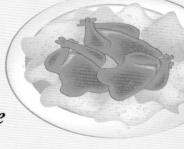

Always washed down by the excellent wines from the surrounding hills, Vicenza's cuisine possesses one legendary dish: the baccalà alla vicentina. *The cod is cooked over a slow flame with garlic, olive oil, anchovies, onion, milk and parmesan cheese. Other specialities of the area include* bigoli con l'anatra *(spaghetti in duck sauce),* pasta and beans alla vicentina, fagioli col cotechino *(beans and pork sausage) and* asparagus risotto. *Various game, generally cooked on a spit, are almost always accompanied by the traditional* polenta. *Another delicious dish is the* paeta rosto, *turkey roasted in pomegranite sauce. In common with the rest of the Veneto region Vicenza too enjoys its* risi e bisi – *rice with peas.*

mullioned windows and balconies adorning its façade.
The visitor to Vicenza will be enthralled by the beauty of its palaces of which there are many others which we do not have the space to list here.

From the Gothic to the Baroque, a tour of sacred art
Vicenza's great churches
From the Gothic cathedral to the art treasures of Santa Corona, from the old basilica of Felice and Fortunato to the Franciscan San Lorenzo

Of all the churches in the Vicenza region, the Domenican **Chiesa di Santa Corona** stands out as the most impressive, containing as it does some fine works of art. Begun in the middle of the 13th century, it contains a thorn from Christ's crown donated by the French king Louis IX. The single-gabled façade has a Romanesque-Gothic structure while the vast and majestic interior has three aisles and is adorned with many chapels. Among the works of art to be found in the church are **Giovanni Bellini**'s *Baptism of Christ* (*Cappella Garzadori*) and the

Adoration of the Magi (1573) by **Paolo Veronese**. Luigi da Porto, author of the famous novella Romeo and Juliet, is buried in the *Cappella Porto* where there are also paintings by **Bartolomeo Montagna**. The *Cappella del Rosario* is magnificent as is the marble inlay work on the 17th century high altar. The *Cappella Valmarana*, through which the crypt is entered, was designed by **Palladio**.
Only slightly less impressive is the very old **Basilica dei martiri santi Felice e Fortunato**, a splendid example of early Christian art

Left: *the church of Santa Corona begun in the 13th century and the Basilica of the saints Felice and Fortunato, which dates back to the 4th century.*

which dates back to 300 AD and preserves the remains of the saints it is named after in the crypt. The architectural history of this church is a saga of many layers – the adjoining **Battistero** and the **Torre campanaria** for example were built later, in the 11th century. For a long period the church belonged to the Benedictine order. It contains early Christian mosaics on its floors, a beautiful apse and a Gothic *tabernacle* by **Antonio da Venezia**. Anyone who loves the charm of old churches should also take a trip to the impressive **Badia di Sant'Agostino** built in the middle of the 1300s on an oratory dating back to the Longobard era. The interior consists of one huge space and on the altar there's an immense 15th century *polyptych* by **Battista da Vicenza** celebrating the meeting between Vicenza and its protector, Venice. It also contains interesting frescoes in the presbytery and two splendid chapels, *Cappella di Cristo Re* and *Cappella della Madonna*.

The Franciscan **Chiesa di San Lorenzo** with its connecting *cloister* has a splendid old Gothic doorway depicting the *Virgin with Child, Saint Francis and Santa Chiara*.

Another church of note is to be found in the Piazza of the same name, **Chiesa di Aracoeli**

which was built in the 17th century on the site of a small pre-existing 13th century church and is one of **Guarino Guarini**'s architectural masterpieces thanks to its rich Baroque façade, adorned with fifteen statues in niches. Inside, there's an impressive Baroque marble *altar* by the 17th century artist **Tommaso Bezzi**.

Finally, the city's most important religious building is the **Cathedral** which rises in Piazza Duomo and is essentially an imposing Gothic structure that has been embellished through the centuries with other styles. It was built on a site where three other churches were known to have existed previously, the first in the 9th century, the second in the 12th and the third in the 14th. The Cathedral is dedicated to Santa Maria Maggiore and its façade (1467) is decorated in white and pink marble with five large arches at the center of which stands a solemn doorway with an 18th century cornice. The interior consists entirely of an immense nave, embellished by seven chapels in one of which can be seen a valuable *polyptych* by **Lorenzo Veneziano**, executed in 1356. A stunning stairway leads up to the *Choir*. The *altar* is the work of **Giovanni da Pademuro** and **Girolamo Pittoni**.

Vicenza's Gothic Duomo: above: the polyptych known as the "Pala d'oro" by Battista da Vicenza preserved in the Badia di Sant'Agostino. Facing page: the 17th century church of Aracoeli and, below, the Badia di Sant'Agostino.

A great artisan tradition
Stones, ceramics and, above all, gold

Vicenza today is the one of the world's centers when it comes to the art of the goldsmith. There are many artisan workshops in Vicenza and craftsmen make

up a notable slice of the local population. The standard of their work benefits from the city's long tradition in the art and the items produced are always of a high quality both in terms of workmanship and style. Two international exhibitions, one dedicated to the goldsmith's art and the other to gemmology, take place every year in Vicenza. The manufacturing of stone enjoys a

long historic tradition in the Vicenza area where it is known as pietra tenera and is used to make statues, fountains and garden ornaments. The entire province is also renowned for its ceramics, especially the pottery from Bassano and Nove where works in earthenware, majolica, stoneware and porcelain are all of excellent quality.

A great Veneto artist from the 1700s

Tiepolo on Vicenza's soil

Though by now in clear political and economic decline, in the 1700s the Venetian Republic and its patricians still committed themselves to the commissioning of splendid works of art; the principle artist of this time was **Giambattista Tiepolo** *(Venice 1696-1770) who, together with his son* **Giandomenico** *and following in the footsteps of Veronese, the great 16th century Veneto artist, has left us a splendid series of frescoes. Especially noteworthy are those adorning the grand staircase and the sala d'onore of the* **Villa Loschi Zileri dal Verme** *where bearded old men, opulent naked women, gods and mythological heroes wheel about in vast skies while Glory, Hunger and*

other virtues enrich the scene. Other significant frescoes can be found in **Villa Cordellina Lombardi**, *near Montecchio Maggiore just outside Vicenza. The real splendor though is to be found in the frescoes in* **Villa Valmarana ai Nani**. *Here the work of Giambattista is contrasted by that of his son Giandomenico who painted the "oriental" rooms and executed scenes of country life. Giambattista, on the other hand, was responsible for the scenes from the Iliad, the Aeneid and Orlando Furioso.*

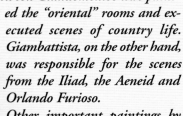

Other important paintings by Tiepolo can be found in the **Chiesa di Santo Stefano** *in Vicenza, in the* **churches of Rampazzo** *and* **Noventa Vicentina** *and in the* **Pinacoteca** *of* **Palazzo Chiericati.**
A collection of drawings from the Tiepolo school are gathered in the **museum in Bassano.**

A fine gallery, a beautiful palace

A showcase for great masters

Since 1855, Vicenza's rich art gallery has been housed in the splendid **Palazzo Chiericati**, in front of which the river Bacchiglione used to flow: this was where ships would drop anchor and markets would be held. Palazzo Chiericati, considered one of **Palladio**'s masterpieces, was only half realized in his lifetime and its completion was entrusted, at the end of the 1600s, to **Carlo Borella**. The palace has a Doric portico on the ground floor and wide lateral loggias on the first floor as well as statues and spires. The interior is decorated with frescoes by **Domenico Ricci**, **Zelotti** and with stuccoes by **Ridolfi**.

The art gallery displays a collection of work by Venetian painters from the 14th and 15th centuries, including **Cima da Conegliano** and **Bartolomeo Montagna**, and works from the great 16th century period of Venetian painting including such illustrious names as **Veronese**, **Tintoretto** and **Jacopo da Bassano**. Venetian artists from the 18th century are also represented with noteworthy masterpieces by artists such as **Giambattista Tiepolo** and **Piazzetta**. The gallery also contains works by European giants such as Memling and the great Van Dyck.

Above: *the* Palazzo Chiericati,
today the home of the Museo Civico.

Above, from left to right: Hans Memling, Crucifixion; Bartolomeo Montagna, Madonna with Child, Magdalene and Saint Monica; Jacopo Bassano, *the* Rectors of Vicenza at the feet of the Virgin; Giambattista Tiepolo, Time Revealing Truth.

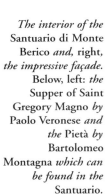

The interior of the Santuario di Monte Berico and, right, the impressive façade. Below, left: the Supper of Saint Gregory Magno by Paolo Veronese and the Pietà by Bartolomeo Montagna which can be found in the Santuario.

Near the city, on the spot where, according to a legend, the Virgin, today venerated in a 15th century statue, appeared to locals

Art and pietà in the Sanctuary del Monte Berico

In the immediate surroundings of Vicenza, enjoying a panoramic view and reached by way of a long portico, lies the **Santuario di Monte Berico** which rises on the spot where, according to tradition, an apparition of the Virgin took place in the 1400s. A small church was built on the site which has steadily been enlarged through the centuries (it is believed that Palladio had a hand in some of its designs). The building which stands today was the work of **Carlo Borella** at the end of the 1600s and is impressive for its three identical façades with sculptures by Orazio Marinali. Inside, at the *high altar*, stands a 15th century colored marble statue of the *Madonna della Misericordia* by **Antonio da Venezia**. On the right of this altar there's the splendid masterpiece of **Bartolomeo Montagna**, la *Pietà*. In the *Refectory* of the connecting convent hangs **Paolo Veronese**'s large painting of the *Supper of St Gregory the Great*.

On the outskirts of Vicenza a supreme Palladian masterpiece

La Rotonda

Half way through the 1500s this cubic construction with its angles pointing in the four cardinal directions to favor light and shadow and a pronaos on every side with six columns preceded by a stairway was erected as a home for a rich canon

Not far from the splendid Villa Valmarana can be found **Palladio**'s true masterpiece – the **Villa Rotonda** – so-called because it describes a circle within a cube. It was built for Paolo Almerico around 1550. The structure is in the form of a cube with its angles perfectly facing the cardinal points, thus allowing splendid effects of light on the façades. Every façade has a pronaos with six columns preceded by wide steps. Three *statues of Francesco Albanese* stand at the top of the tympanum. Inside, the main hall mirrors the idea of the circle inscribed inside the cube. The *cupola* of the Rotonda was built by **Vincenzo Scamozzi**. An elaborate winding staircase connects the very lavishly decorated state apartment to the ground floor which was the servants quarters. The central hall is decorated with frescoes by Dorigny, executed in the 17th century, some time after the villa had been built. Of the three thousand or so villas in Veneto, the Rotonda, also known as **Villa Capra**, is without question the jewel in the crown.

Two images of Palladio's absolute masterpiece: Villa La Rotonda *built in the middle of the 16th century for Paolo Almerico.*

Villa Valmarana "ai Nani"

*Linked to a curious old story, this splendid villa,
near the city, owned by the Valmarana family for three centuries,
hosted and engaged the talents of two great artists, father and son,
Giambattista and Giandomenico Tiepolo*

On the vast stretch of land owned by the Valmarana family, stands **Villa Valmarana ai Nani**, attributed to **Antonio Muttoni** at the end of the 1600s. It gets its name, Nani, which means dwarfs, because of a curious legend. A dwarf child was born to the noble proprietor. So as to prevent the child from realizing its handicap, the master of the house surrounded her with dwarf servants. But one day, the girl child looked out of a window and saw a handsome knight riding a horse. She immediately understood her infirmity and killed herself. The servants all turned to stone and, ac-

cording to the legend, are the statues which today adorn the villa.

Apart from its stunning architectural qualities – the wide colonnade, the stables, the garden and the terraced façade – the villa is famous for housing the 18th century frescoes of **Giambattista Tiepolo** and, to a lesser extent, his son, **Giandomenico**. The great master depicts scenes from the *Iliad*, the *Aeneid* and *Orlando Furioso* while his son, with a touch of irony, limits himself to scenes of country life, including a group of Veneto peasants sharing a picnic in the open air.

Veneto cuisine: recipes

Fish dishes

SARDINES IN VINEGAR (SARDELE IN SAOR). *Remove head, backbone and entrails of the sardines and clean them. Cover in flour and fry in boiling olive oil. Place them on kitchen roll and salt them. Place back on the stove and add half a glass of olive oil. Add a chopped onion and two glasses of vinegar and let cook for a few minutes. Arrange the sardines in layers in a bowl and add the hot vinegar and the onion together with some pine nuts and raisins. The sardines should now be left to marinate in the vinegar which should last a day or two.*

INGREDIENTS (SERVES FOUR PEOPLE). 600 grams of fresh sardines; 50 grams of pine nuts; 50 grams of raisins; 2 onions; white flour; vinegar; olive oil and salt.

CRAB (GRANSEOLA). *Place the crabs in a saucepan of boiling water and cook for about ten minutes (granseola is a large species of crab commonly found in the Adriatic and favoured by the people of Veneto). When they have cooled down extract them from their shells. Set aside the shells on the serving dish. Chop up the crab meat and season with salt, pepper and a tablespoon or two of olive oil and lemon juice. Now return the crab meat to the shells and garnish with parsley.*

INGREDIENTS (SERVES FOUR). 4 crabs; salt; olive oil; lemon juice; pepper and parsley.

EEL (BISATO IN TECIA). *Pour half a liter of vinegar in a bowl and add a few bay leaves, salt and pepper into which place the washed eels and leave to marinate for a few hours. Cover the eels in breadcrumbs and place in a frying pan with a knob of butter, two tablespoons of olive oil and two segments of garlic. Brown the eels and then soak them in vinegar and a small glass of marsala wine. Once the eels have absorbed the liquid, add some tomato puré diluted in hot water. Garnish with salt and pepper and cook for a long time. Add some parsley to the cooked eels and, if possible, a few slices of polenta.*

INGREDIENTS (SERVES FOUR). 1kg of eels; bay leaves; vinegar; salt; pepper; breadcrumbs; garlic; butter; olive oil; white wine; tomato puré and parsley.

SHELLFISH (CAPE SANTE). *Clean the shellfish and place them in a frying pan with oil over a strong flame. As soon as they've opened, remove them from their shell. Cover them in breadcrumbs and continue coking, adding garlic, parsley and a little olive oil and butter. Add white wine and few drops of lemon juice and, when ready, return them to their shells and serve.*

INGREDIENTS (SERVES FOUR PEOPLE). 12 shellfish; olive oil, garlic; parsley; breadcrumbs; butter; white wine and lemon juice.

An evocative view of Bassano with its famous Ponte Vecchio. Below: aerial view of Bassano del Grappa.

BASSANO DEL GRAPPA

A pretty town of arcaded streets and frescoed palaces, rich in crafts and culture. Home of a great artist and world center of grappa

Monte Grappa, sacred to Italy

Dominating the city of Bassano and the towns of the Valsugana, **Monte Grappa** is held dear in the memory of patriotic Italians for it was here that, during the First World War, many bloody and decisive battles were fought wit the Austro-Hungarian forces. The fighting took place in the winter of 1917, and then in June and October of 1918. The grave defeat of Caporetto was to follow before the Italians finally came out on the winning side in the war. A shrine to the soldiers who fought here has been set up on the mount and contains memorabilia regarding the war.

There are three things you should do first on arriving in Bassano: stroll across **Ponte Vecchio**, an old wooden bridge famous throughout the world and dear to the locals; visit the splendid **Pinacoteca**, an art gallery containing many masterpieces of painting; and drink a glass of the local grappa.

Ponte Vecchio is a covered wooden bridge which has been destroyed and rebuilt many times in the course of history, always though with a careful eye on recreating the original design of the great **Andrea Palladio** (1569). It was last rebuilt in 1948 and has since taken on the name **Ponte degli Alpini**. It is made of wood because wood is more resistant to the force of the river's current than stone. Another place of interest in Bassano is the **Museo Civico**. This museum is endowed with an interesting archaeological section, exhibiting finds from pre-Christian civilizations right through to the late medieval period. The adjoining **Museo della Ceramica** (in **Palazzo Sturm**) is also well worth a visit for its fine displays of ceramics. We then come to the Pinacoteca, the art gallery on the first floor of the Museo Civico which contains the most important works of the town's most famous son, **Jacopo Dal Ponte**, known as **Bassano** (see inset on facing page). Other interesting works in the gallery include the 14th century *Stational Cross* by **Guariento**, the 14th century *Madonna with Child* by **Michele Giambono** and 15th century works by **Antonio** and **Bartolomeo Vivarini**. Venetian art is well represented by the works of **Giambattista** and **Giandomenico Tiepolo**, **Alessandro Magnasco**, **Giovanbattista Piazzetta** and **Pietro Longhi**. There are also two rooms dedicated to

The masterpieces in the "Pinacoteca"
Jacopo, great artist of the 1500s

The Museo Civico in Bassano *contains many of the works by* Jacopo da Bassano, *the great painter who was born and, between 1510 and 1592, had a workshop in the town. He came from a family of painters, the Dal Pontes, and his father Francesco il Vecchio was a well-respected artist in his own right. His son Jacopo however was the more talented and was to become the more famous. The masterpieces of his on display at* the Museo Civico include the **Adoration** *(see photo),* Lamenting the Dead Christ, Baptism of St Lucilla, Flight into Egypt, the Martyring of St Catherine *and* Saint John the Baptist. *Jacopo was an exponent, to some extent, of the Lombardy naturalistic school and also fell under the influence of Pordenone. Essentially though he was influenced by northern art and the mannerist schools. His paintings are distinguished by the wide range of tonal values he employs.*

19th and 20th century works.

Of prehistoric origins, Bassano has been ruled by various masters through the centuries: the Ezzelini, the della Scala, the Carraresi and the Visconti families all having enjoyed a spell of power here. At the beginning of the 1400s it passed into the hands of the Venetian Republic. Bassano is thus characterized by a variety of different architectural and artistic styles, the prime example of which is probably provided by the many palaces whose façades are sometimes frescoed by fine artists. Having visited the **Duomo**, the *Campanile* (built from one of the castle's towers), the **Torre degli Ezzelini** and the **Castello superiore** with its large Romanesque portal, one should then inspect the most beautiful example of Baroque architecture in Bassano – Palazzo Sturm in Via Schivanetti. Built in 1750 and looking out over the River Brenta, it is a seven-storeyed building whose terraces descend down onto the river. Inside, there are splendid frescoes and stuccoes. The heart of Bassano though remains the old **Piazza dei Signori**, dominated by the beautiful 16th century **Palazzo Municipale** and its older **Loggia**.

An exceptional car museum

In Romano d'Ezzelino, not far from Bassano, there's a museum, perhaps the only one of its kind in the whole of Europe, which is dedicated to automobiles. It's called the **Museo Luigi Bonfanti**. The unique aspect of the museum is that every six months it completely changes not only its exhibits but also its decor and structure. Founded in recent years by the great car enthusiast and collector who gives the museum its name, it is endowed with a splendid archive and, among many other things, exhibits the "Lauro" car, built in 1889 and one of the most interesting models still in existence in the world today.

The Museo dell'Automobile. Left: Flight into Egypt *by* Jacopo da Bassano.

Sampling the food on offer
On the table in Bassano

Sitting down to a meal in Bassano, the first dish to ask for is a big helping of *white asparagus*. In season in April and May, these asparagus are distinguished by the way in which they are cultivated and have become popular outside Italy. Bassano dedicates several fairs every year to the asparagus, such is its notoriety in the area. You might also want to sample a plate of *radicchio variegato*, the true speciality of the nearby Castelfranco. The other great dishes renowned in this area include *pollo alla cacciatora* (chicken), *zuppe di trippa* (a tripe soup) and *baccalà with polenta*. As a starter you might like to try the *sopressa*, a tasty pork sausage not dissimilar to salami.

A rich and various crop of vegetables flourishes in the soil in the environs around Bassano including peas, broccoli, various herbs and dif-

ferent varieties of beans and thus the produce is always fresh and wholesome in the town. Bassano also takes great pride in its sweet things. Desserts worth sampling include the *pinsa*, (a cake made with cornmeal and white flour) and *zaleti* (again cakes made with cornmeal).

As for wines, the area produces some excellent Doc certified brands. Recommended are the *Breganze bianco*, the *Malvasia Campo dei Fiori* and the excellent *prosecco*. The are also produces some high quality red wines.

One of Italy's great institutions, grappa, *might have its reign in Veneto but its throne surely sits in Bassano. Grappa is a distillation of marc, a refuse of pressed grapes. Bassano contains a series of historical distilleries where grappa has been made for centuries. In order to understand the history and making of grappa better you can visit the* Museo della Grappa *in the town or the many renowned* grapperie *around Ponte Vecchio, including the old "Bottega" in the vicinity of Ponte degli Alpini.*

The great grappa of Bassano

In olden times, the landowners kept the wine for themselves, leaving the marc for the workers. By distilling the

marc however the contadini produced the "graspa" or grappa as it is known as today. Its origins date back to around the 12th century. For a long period grappa was also served as a medicinal drink.

The European Union has granted a certification to grappa only in Italy, a testament to its long tradition in the country. There are various kinds of grappa – the young grappas, grappas matured in wooden containers, old grappas, flavored grappas and grappa di monovitigno.

An image of Piazza della Libertà, *once Piazza dei Signori.*

A traditional and famous industry
Old and new ceramics

Bassano and the nearby Nove have been producing splendid ceramics for centuries. This craft in fact can be traced back to the 1600s in the area. Among the most renowned workshops in the 1700s was the one owned by the Antonibon *family and a member of this family,* Giovanni Battista Antonibon, *produced plates and crockery of such high quality that his work became famous and led to the opening of shops in other cities. The pottery produced by the innumerable artisan workshops in Bassano is always distinguished by its exceptionally high standard of craftsmanship and in the neighboring Nove the displays of ceramics in the many shop windows pay testament to this fact.*

Anyone wanting to investigate further into this art which has other important centers in Italy like Faenza and Florence, would do well to visit the Museo Storico della Ceramica *and the* Museo Civico della Ceramica. *Both of these fasci-* nating museums can be found between Bassano and Nove. It's worth remembering that, although a vibrant agricultural center, Bassano is also a town with a rich and varied tradition in the crafts. Once upon a time, it was a thriving center for seamstresses and weavers of wool and silk; artisan workshops than sprang up that specialized in fine ornate furniture which still today enjoys an international fame. There is also a thriving goldsmiths tradition who today specialize in the making of gold chains. Another craft at which the artisans of Bassano have excelled for centuries is printing, *begun by the famous family of typographers, the* Remondini.

Those life-size chess pieces
Marostica

Beautiful town, famous for its cherries and its historical chess game

Right: *the charming Piazza Chilesotti in Thiene.* Below, right: *Thiene's Duomo.*

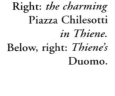

The historical "Partita a scacchi" played in the piazza of Marostica. Below: *pieces of the chess game.*

If you happen to be in Marostica in June don't lose the opportunity to pay a visit to the cherry fair *held in the town every year to showcase the extreme high quality of its home-grown fruit. And while you're there you might also want to try the* bigoli con l'anatra *(pasta with duck) which is a local speciality. If on the other hand you happen to find yourself in Marostica in September of an even-numbered year you'll enjoy the rare treat of witnessing the well-known historical* chess game *when human figures take the place of the chess pieces and the game is carried out in the main piazza. This spectacular tradition goes back as far as 1454 and involves as many as 500 participants. It would appear that the Humanist Taddeo Pariso, father of a beautiful daughter who two knights were courting, invited the two suitors to play a game of chess rather than fight for his daughter's hand. Other points of interest in Marostica include the Scaligera walls, the remains of* Castello Superiore, *perched above the town and, below, the battlemented* Castello Inferiore, *today home of the town council. In the* church of Sant'Antonio *there's a 16th century altarpiece of* St Paul in Athens *by* Francesco *and* Jacopo Bassano.

At the foot of the high plains of Asiago
Thiene

Medieval town known for the beautiful Villa da Porto-Colleoni, one of the most impressive in Veneto

On the Asiago plain, twenty kilometers from Vicenza, stands the small elegant old town of Thiene which begun its life as a Roman settlement, then became Longobard until, in the 1400s, falling under the aegis of the Venice Republic. The splendid cas-

tle, known as the **Villa da Porto-Colleoni** was built in the 1400s in a late Venetian Gothic style. It contains frescoed rooms by **Veronese**, **Fasolo** and **G.B. Zelotti**. The 18th century stables are impressive, where the original large marble-floored enclosure and its 36 columns surmounted by putti and the antique wooden manger have all been well-preserved.

Other sights to see in Thiene include the 17th century *Campanile* of Serlio, the 15th century **Chiesa della Natività di Maria Vergine**; the **Duomo** with interesting paintings by **Sebastiano Ricci**, and the 17th century Baroque **Chiesa del Rosario**. The **Chiesa di San Vicenzo** is the oldest religious building in the town.

RECOARO
Amidst the enchantment of the mountains the well-being of thermal baths

Recoaro sits ten kilometers from Valdagno in the enchanting "emerald shell" beneath the mountains known as the Small Dolomites *(a cablecar service operates in the winter for skiers). Above all though, Recoaro is celebrated for its hot springs. The first thermal baths were, in fact, built as far back as 1780 and by the end of the 19th century it had become a fashionable international spa center.*

Today Recoaro is blessed with nine springs, five of which are within the thermal baths complex, itself nestled inside a vast park. The others – Franco, Aureliana, Capitello and Giuliana – are all to be found in the near surroundings and all possess special healing properties. The small elegant town with its Liberty-style architecture offers various therapeutic services including mud baths and in itself deserves to be seen for the splendor and peace of the beautiful surroundings of its idyllic location.

Schio and Valdagno: textile havens

About thirty kilometers from Vicenza, surrounded by mountains, including the towering Pasubio, nestles the small town of Valdagno which is among the chief wool manufacturers in Italy. Here it was in 1836 that Luigi Marzotto (head of a powerful industrial family which still exerts its influence today) installed the first wool plant. Standing out among all the numerous large factories there's the 17th century **Villa Valle-Marzotto**, now the home of the local council, and a palaeontological museum.

If it was the Marzottis who brought prosperity to Valdagno, the nearby Schio, with its 40,000 inhabitants, owes its wealth to the Rossi, also wool merchants, who, in the middle of the 19th century, could already count on the services of a thousand employees. Earlier still, at the beginning of the 1700s, when Schio was under the power of the Venice Republic, the town had become an important textile center.

Military city on Paduan soil with a city wall still in tact

Cittadella

Built as a military stronghold by Paduan forces who were at war with Treviso and under threat from the nearby Castelfranco which the enemy armies had taken, Cittadella was suddenly created in 1220. Built on an artificial earthwork with a large moat, Cittadella has an imposing appearance enforced by its polygonal walls (1500 meters long and 13 meters high), thirty two towers and three immense gates (from within, next to **Porta Padova**, rises the **Torre di Malta**). Within its walls, Cittadella is built around a right-angled streetplan with two roads known as *stradelle* acting as the main axis. The neo-classical **Duomo**, built on the site of an old church, is of interest as are the **Palazzetto Municipale**, the **theater** with its neo-classical façade and the 16th century **Palazzo Pretorio**.

On the Paduan plains a jewel enclosed inside its medieval walls

Montagnana

Born, like Cittadella, from military requirements, Montagnana – also like Cittadella belonging to the province of Padua though it lies between Padua and Vicenza – possesses three points of real interest: the old walls, erected by Padua's ruler, **Ubertino da Carrara** around the middle of the 1300s; the splendid vast Piazza Maggiore, the city's center; and the magnificent **Duomo** dedicated to Maria Assunta and built between 1431 and 1502 with a contribution from the entire populace of the town. Paying testament to its long military history are the remains, towards Porta Padova, of the **Castello di San Zeno** and, near Porta Legnago, the **Rocca degli Alberi**. Also worthy of note is the Palladian **Palazzo dei Pisani** (1552).

Panorama of Schio with the Duomo.

Panorama of the city of the Scaligeras taken from the Roman theater. Facing page: the celebrated Piazza Bra with its legendary "Listone" and the old Roman amphitheater. Below, left: Palazzo della Gran Guardia Right: the neo-classical Palazzo Barbieri Below: the fountain in Piazza Bra.

Here's the city

Nestling among soft hills against a backdrop of mountains near Lake Garda and served by a stately river, Verona, the second largest city in Veneto, combines a splendid natural location with a rich history and a vibrant agricultural and cultural industry (museums, libraries, a university). A variety of styles co-exist harmoniously in Verona: Roman, Gothic, Medieval and neo-classical palaces, walls and towers all jostle for attention within the city's walls. And, adding an air of romance to this small and vibrant city, it was of course the setting for Shakespeare's most romantic and famous drama – the tale of the two star-crossed lovers, *Romeo and Juliet*.

On a more contemporary note, Verona also holds large fairs and exhibitions every year, like the **International Agricultural Fair**, the **Samoter**, or the **International farming machinery show**.

VERONA

Romanesque, medieval, neo-classical, situated in a splendid geographical location, Verona is famous for its Arena, the story of Romeo and Juliet, the kindness of its inhabitants and its delicious food, not least of all the famous Pandoro.

Three piazzas, the heart of the city

Like Padua, the central core of Verona is essentially made up of three vibrant piazzas all of which combine the gentle vitality of the Veronese character with the solemn and harmonious nature of the city's architecture. **Piazza Bra**, besides being Verona's largest and one of the most architecturally significant piazzas in Italy, is perhaps the liveliest and most sociable of the three. No less vibrant and perhaps a little more picturesque though, is **Piazza delle Erbe**, which is animated every day by a fruit and vegetable market and ennobled by its stately architectural splendours. **Piazza dei Signori**, on the other hand, is radical-

NOT TO BE MISSED
- *The Arena* ● *San Zeno*
- *Romeo and Juliet, what remains*

DISHES AND WINES TO SAMPLE
- *Risi and bisi* ● *Zuppa scaligera*
- *Pandoro* ● *Valpolicella* ● *Soave*

CRAFTS
- *Wrought iron* ● *Gold*

PANORAMAS OF THE CITY
- *Strada dei colli* ● *Strada delle Torricelle* ● *Ponte di Castelvecchio*

ENVIRONS
- *Bardolino* ● *Lazise* ● *Castelli Scaligeri* ● *Lake Garda*

ly different – stately and aristocratic, it is known as Verona's "salon". But let's start with Piazza Bra on our tour of the city. Verona's largest piazza is reached by passing through the *Bra Gates*, the two crenelated arches that form part of the old wall circling the city which was built by **Gian Galeazzo Visconti** in the 14th century.

Irregular in shape, Piazza Bra (whose name probably derives from "braida", a northern term for plain or field) is lined with prestiguous buildings on three of its sides among which stand out, on the right of the arches, the **Palazzo della Gran Guardia**, built in 1610 by **Domenico Curtoni** (but completed only at

The "Liston"

The "Listone" in Piazza Bra is the legendary meeting place of the Veronese when they go out for their afternoon stroll. It is in fact merely a stretch of sidewalk which follows the curve of one of Piazza Bra's sides and is flanked by elegant arcades, shops and cafes. Anyone who truly wants to enter into the spirit of Verona should, after having seen the sights, take the time to stroll along the "Listone".

the beginning of the 1800s). On another of its sides, there's the neo-classical **Palazzo Barbieri** (where the municipality has its headquarters), a grandiose imitation of old Roman temples which was built in 1838.
Following the curve of the other side of the piazza we find a number of stately palaces, most of which are arcaded and enlivened by cafes and elegant shops. Here is where we find the legendary *Listone* (or Liston). This is the large promenade favored by the Veronese for their daily stroll.

The Maffei Museum

The **Maffei Museum** houses a collection of tombstones, inscriptions, statues and funeral urns of notable importance from both the Roman and Medieval times and was the first museum of its kind in Europe, having been founded in 1714 by the Veronese **Scipione Maffei**. For a more astute understanding of the Roman aspect of Verona with its **Arena** and the **Arco dei Gavi**, a visit here is obligatory.

The Arena, a 1000 year-old miracle

Aerial view of the Arena. The huge Roman amphitheater which dominates the city of Verona.

THE THIRD LARGEST ROMAN AMPHITHEATER

● *Elipitical in shape, the amphitheater which has been passed down to us virtually in tact from antiquity, is 139 metres long and 110 metres wide. It was built in the first century AD.*

● *In Roman times, when it accomodated almost the entire population of the city, it hosted gladiator fights which were invariably fought to the death.*

● *The Arena possesses 44 rows of seats and is endowed with underground cages where the lions and other wild beasts were kept.*

On Piazza Bra, the vast and lively meeting place of the Veronese, towers the the old Roman amphitheater known as the **Arena** which was built, in those days outside the city walls, in the first century AD and which is the largest of the monuments of antiquity apart from the Colosseum and the Amphitheater in Capua.

The imposing building was built during the reigns of Augustus and Claudius and consists of blocks of Veronese stone. It's more than 30 metres high in the center ring and is one of the best preserved buildings of antiquity we still possess.

At the time of its construction it would appear that the Amphitheater accomodated the entire Roman population of the city. Early entertainments enacted there included simulat-

ed battles, gladiator fights and bullfights but it was also where capital punishments were carried out.

Since 1580 the protection of the amphitheater has been entrusted to a special magistracy. At the beginning of this century it became the venue for a yearly opera festival which is famous throughout the world and attracts artists of the highest calibre.

Verdi's Aida *on the large stage of the Arena.* Inset: *mosaic depicting gladiators and a portrait of* G. Verdi.

From Roman gladiators to Giuseppe Verdi's Aida

Ever since it was built, in the first century AD, the **Arena** has been the venue for all kinds of events and entertainments and is mentioned in the works of the historian Pliny the Younger.

In Roman times the arena staged gladiators fights where soldiers fought against each other and with savage beasts.

In medieval times jousts and tornaments were held there as well as circus acts and bullfights (one of which was witnessed by Napoleon in 1805).

The many memorable events to have taken place in the Arena includes the staging of **Gioacchino Rossini**'s opera, the *Sacred Alliance*, in 1822.

The world-famous opera season held every summer in the Arena began in August 1913 with a performance of **Verdi**'s *Aida*.

UNESCO has recently awarded Verona the title of "world capital of opera and poetry" because of its initiatives in this field and its power of attracting music lovers from all over the world.

and the imposing **Palazzo Maffei** with its loggia and statues of pagan divinities. By its side stands the **Torre del Gardello**, a tower built entirely with bricks at the behest of **Cansignorio della Scala**. On the north east side of the piazza rises the **Casa Mazzanti** with beautiful frescoes by A. Cavalli, the **Domus Nova** and the **Palazzo del Comune**. The piazza also flaunts the city's tallest tower: the **Torre dei Lamberti** which is 33 metres high.
At the heart of the piazza, stands the 16th cen-

Piazza delle Erbe

Two views of Piazza delle Erbe *and two details of the piazza with the* Edicola *and the* Column with St Mark's Lion.

We have already alluded to the vibrant and colorful nature of this piazza, which is often referred to as Verona's most beautiful monument; now it's time to study it in a little more detail beginning with the crenelated and arcaded 14th century **Domus Mercatorum**

tury column with St Mark's Lion as a testament to the old days of Venetian rule, the *Fountain of the Verona Madonna*, commissioned by Cansignorio in 1368 with its Roman statuary and the elegant 16th century building known as the **Berlina** which was used for the investiture of public magistrates. Finally, there's the 15th century *tabernacle*.

When hunger calls, here's a speciality to try
Brasato all'Amarone

Seated in one of Verona's excellent and elegant restaurants and eager to sample a mouth-watering local speciality, you could do no better than order a **brasato all'Amarone**.
It's a large piece of veal marinated in Amarone wine from Valpolicella and a variety of vegetables. It should be cooked slowly and served cut into strips with a light vegetable sauce. You can rest assured that, once enjoyed, brasato all'Amarone will remain one of your favorite memories of Verona.

The famous balcony of Juliet's house. Below, left: the presumed tomb of the heroine; a statue of her in bronze (N. Costantini); the house where, according to legend, Romeo lived.

The great Veronese love affair immortalized by Shakespeare
Romeo and Juliet: two houses, one balcony

To begin with it was a legend originating in Siena which Masuccio Salernitano drew on for one of his fifty novellas. However, in the following century, a writer from Vicenza, Luigi Da Porto, moved the story to Verona. His novella, entitled Romeo and Juliet, was written in 1525. A soldier and a man of letters, Da Porto conceived much of the story which Shakespeare was to elaborate and immortalize. In a 14th century Verona ruled by Bartolomeo della Scala, the two young lovers, Romeo Montecchi and Juliet Capuleti were in love but the rift between their families caused by Romeo having accidentally killed one of Juliet's cousins made it impossible for the two lovers to happily marry and finally led to their tragic deaths. This perfect story of love and death soon enjoyed a worldwide fame and poets of every country wrote their own versions. But it was William Shakespeare, with his tragedy, Romeo and Juliet (1591 or 1595) who was to finally immortalize the story.

In **Via delle Arche Scaligere**, there's a medieval house made of old crenelated bricks which, so legend has it, was once the home of the **Montecchi** family, to which **Romeo** belonged. The building now is in a state of disrepair. On the other hand, one can still enter the courtyard of the other famous home, that which legend ascribes to **Juliet** of the **Capuleti** family. Juliet's house can be found in **Via Cappello**, near Piazza delle Erbe. It's another 13th century townhouse. In the inner courtyard, which has recently been restored and is a site of pilgrimage for romantic tourists from all over the world, stands Juliet's famous **balcony**. There are also some verses from Shakespeare in marble in both English and Italian. A modern statue of the heroine in bronze and her presumed *tomb* complete Verona's tribute to the most famous lovers in the world.

The organ on which Mozart played

Something not to be missed is the organ in **St Thomas' church**, a stupendous baroque instrument of exceptional sound quality. In 1717, on this organ, the best of its kind in Verona, **Wolfgang Amadeus Mozart** held a concert which attracted music lovers from far and wide. Mozart, in fact,

had already been to Verona when he was a mere thirteen-year old. This church, dedicated to St Thomas Beckett, also houses a second musical instrument of note – a contro organ in the choir. It would appear however that neither instrument has been put to use for a very long time.

Above: Porta Bombardiera, in the courtyard of Palazzo del Capitano. Right: the elegant Piazza dei Signori with its monument to Dante and, left: the splendid 15th century Loggia del Consiglio.

The harmonious aristocracy of Piazza dei Signori

Adjacent to Piazza delle Erbe but more stately and harmonious, we find Piazza dei Signori which is reached through the *Arco della Costa* (whose name is derived from the whale rib which, curiously, can be found underneath). At the heart of this impressive piazza stands the 19th century *statue of Dante* by **Ugo Zannoni**. Though more worthy of attention perhaps are the wonders which surround it, first and foremast of which is constituted by the extremely elegant **Loggia del Consiglio** (built in the second half of the 15th century) whose Tuscan sobriety is compensated by its warm and colorful decoration making it perhaps the most evocative of the buildings of the Veronese Renaissance. It is ornamented by a series of statues around the cornice representing Catullus, Pliny, Vitruvius and Cornelius Nepote.

Palazzo del Comunale with its Romanesque façade and renaissance embellishments is made of both stone and bricks and also on the

same piazza you'll find the 15th century *Scala della Ragione*. Facing the piazza you'll also come across the **Palazzo del Capitano** with its 14th century courtyard where the **Loggia Barbaro** and the *Portale* are both of great interest. It is now the courthouse.

For a moment of relaxation the Caffè Dante is worth a visit with its unique 18th century elegance.

The Scaligera tombs, the culmination of the Gothic in Verona

Near Piazza dei Signori stands the small Romanesque **church of Santa Maria Antica**, the resting place of Verona's Scaligera family. The tombs of the Scaligera family, known as the *Arche Scaligere*, are among the most impressive in Italy. At the entrance of the church, stands the *tomb of Cangrande I* (1329) with its solemn and reclining sculpture of the dead nobleman. Cangrande also features in the splendid, large *Statua Equestre* (a copy of the original which is now in Castelvecchio), a genuine masterpiece of 13th century sculpture.

The other Scaligera tombs, protected by an iron gate, are next to the church (*see inset*).

Here lay the *Signori* of Verona

Inside the marble enclosure and the wrought iron gate which carries the emblem of the *Scala*, we find the other Scaligera tombs, many of which are in the form of sarcophaguses, the most impressive of which is perhaps the *Arca di Mastino II* (1351) – raised up on columns, the equestrian statue of the prince is supported on a pyramid and contained within a Gothic baldachin. Other works of note include the splendidly decorated **tomb of Cansignorio** (1375), executed by **Bonino da Campione** and **Gaspare Broaspini.**

Above, left: *the* Tomb of Cangrande *and his* Equestrian statue.
Below, left: *the* Arca di Cansignorio *and a detail from his* Equestrian statue.

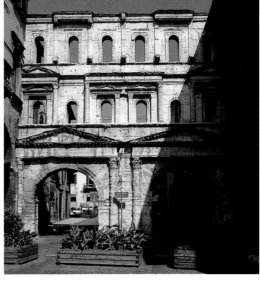

Where history has been made

Above: the old Arco dei Gavi, near the river Adige. At he end of the old Decumanus rises Porta Borsari, the barrel-vaulted Roman gate.

Near the Adige, in the gardens skirting the castle at Castelvecchio, rises the **Arco dei Gavi**, a triumphal first century Roman arch constructed in honor of the Gavi family. Destroyed by the French in 1805 and re-built in 1932, this arch is a wonderful testament to the days of the Roman Empire.

Another vestige of ancient Rome is the barrel-vaulted **Porta Borsari**, perhaps the best-preserved ancient monument in Verona. The door, dating back to the first century B.C, was inserted into the wall and still today displays elegant tympanums, columns and a double row of windows. It's not difficult to see how this style of architecture was to later influence the creators of Renaissance Verona.

For anyone wanting to visit and know Verona in its essence and entirety, it's also worthwhile pointing out two old entrances to the city: **Porta Nuova**, a solemn and elegant construction commissioned by **Michele Sanmicheli** around the middle of the 15th century which leads directly to the center of the city; and **Portoni della Bra**, two large crenelated arches, built into the old city walls, which lead straight into the huge and lively Piazza Bra.

Culinary specialities

Buon appetito in Verona

Veronese cuisine, in common with the entire Veneto region, has a sumptuous tradition to fall back on and boasts a variety of gastronomical specialities.

In Verona, as is the case in the rest of the region, the local speciality is the celebrated Risi and Bisi – *consisting of rice and peas which, as mentioned, formed the first part of the doge's lunch at the festival of St Marks (see the Rice Report). Rice and peas are the ingredients of many other soups as, for example, the excellent* Minestrone di Tagliatelle *which honors in particular the festival of San Zeno. Also recommended are the* Risotto all'ochetta *and* the Risotto alla pilota.

Utterly Veronese is the exquisite dish known as Zuppa alla Scaligera *whose recipe dates back to the times of Cangrande della Scala. Another historical dish is the* Petti di pollo alla Mastino della Scala.

A good lunch in Verona might be gotten underway with a mouth-watering starter consisting of, for example, Salame all'aglio, *a local speciality. To finish off the lunch why not sample some of the excellent Veneto cheeses, in particular,* Asiago, Provolone *or* Castella. *A good radicchio from Treviso or Chioggia will help to being out the flavor of the cheese. You might then enjoy a pear or a peach from the Verona countryside or even a slice of* Pandoro.

Crafts

The refined and extensive Veneto tradition where objects in wrought iron are concerned finds its capital in Verona. Other interesting centers include Castelmassa and the Polesine region. Still today one can find splendid articles manufactured in wrought iron including railings, gates,

fireplaces and lamps. In fact, there's an international academy of iron in Mogliano, in the province of Treviso where masters and students from all over the world carry out their craft.

Above: *the immense 13th century* castle of Castelvecchio *which today houses Verona's most important museum.*
Below: *the* Ponte Scaligero, *part of the Castelvecchio complex from where one can enjoy a splendid panorama of the Adige and the city.*

Castelvecchio, a museum full of masterpieces

Hosting of one of the most important and lavishly endowed museums of Europe, **Castello di San Martino in Acquario** – the complex known as **Castelvecchio** – is a large fortified turreted castle built into the ancient walls at the behest of Cangrande II della Scala in the middle of the 1400s. The imposing castle witnessed a series of battles during the ensuing centuries and possesses six towers, including the main tower known as the **Mastio**.
A crenelated wall runs around the perimeter

house constructed by Napoleon and restored at the beginning of the century.
The fortress can be said to be divided into two distinct blocks: on the one side, there's the *Reggia*, the residence of the Della Scala family and on the other, *Piazza d'Armi*. From the castle one reaches the bridge called **Ponte Scaligero**, an impressive construction consisting of three differently shaped arches made of brick which was destroyed during the Second World War but swiftly re-built using all the original materials.
In the sixties, this extraordinary bridge benefitted from expert restoration carried out by the great Venetian architect **Carlo Scarpa**.

accompanied by a deep moat which was once filled with water from the Adigetto. Inside, there are three differently shaped courtyards, the old **church of San Martino** and a block-

By paying a visit to the castle and its environs, one prepares oneself for the wealth of treasures contained in the museum on the premises.

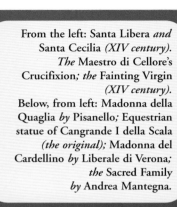

What to see at the Castelvecchio Museum

In these fundamental museum which covers many centuries of art, there's a fine collection of Romanesque sculpture from the 12th and 13th centuries and Veronese sculpture from the 14th century (Santa Caterina, Santa Cecilia, Santa Martha, the Throned Madonna with Child and Saint Libera). Not to be missed are the large Crucifixion and the group of Maria and Martha by the **Maestro di Cellore** from the late 1300s.

The museum also houses a large collection of Veronese bells and old weapons as well as 12th and 13th century frescoes which have been removed from various churches and palaces of the city.

Room XI contains **Jacopo Bellini**'s *Madonna dell'Umiltà, Saint Jerome* and *the Risen Christ*. Other masterpieces to be found in this room include **Pisanello**'s *Madonna della quaglia* and two works by **Stefano da Verona**, the *Madonna del Roseto* and a *Madonna with Child*.

Passing through the rooms exhibiting works by foreign artists such as **Pietro Paolo Rubens** one arrives in Room XIII, where a *crucifix* by **Jacopo Bellini**, the *Death of the Virgin* by **Giambono** and various works by **Giovanni Badile** including the *Polittico dell'Aquila* are displayed. After a series of works from the Veronese Re-

From the left: Santa Libera *and* Santa Cecilia *(XIV century)*. *The* Maestro di Cellore's Crucifixion; *the* Fainting Virgin *(XIV century)*. Below, from left: Madonna della Quaglia *by* Pisanello; Equestrian statue of Cangrande I della Scala *(the original)*; Madonna del Cardellino *by* Liberale di Verona; *the* Sacred Family *by* Andrea Mantegna.

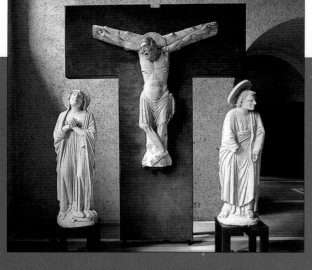

naissance displayed in Room XIV, the next room contains works by the great Venetian masters of the Renaissance and thus merits especial attention. Here you'll find two stupendous *Madonnas with Child* both by **Giovanni Bellini**, *Two Saints with Page* by **Vittore Carpaccio** and other interesting works by **Bartolomeo Montagna**. Room XVI contains paintings by **Domenico** and **Francesco Morone**.

In the next room there's a stupendous *Madonna and Child* by **Francesco Bonsignori**.

Room XVIII contains fine works by **Liberale da Verona**, including the *Madonna del Cardellino*, the Adoration of the Shepherds and an impressive Crib.

Room XIX is dominated by the *Sacred Family* by **Andrea Mantegna**. Other works here by the same artist include *Christ Carrying the Cross* and *Madonna with Child and Santa Juliana*. This large museum also contains the original of the equestrian statue of *Cangrande I*, removed from the Scaligere Tombs where now stands a copy.

In the remaining rooms works which merit special attention include the splendid panels by **Caroto**, *Giovane Monaco* and the *Young Boy with Drawing*, a *Madonna Maffei* by **Girolamo Dai Libri** and the *Deposition* by **Paolo Veronese**. **Jacopo Tintoretto** is represented with works including *Concert of the Muses* and *Adoration of the Shepherds*. Later works by Veneto artists include two *Capricci* by Guardi and *Tre Camaldolesi and Santa Teresa* by **Giovan Battista Tiepolo**.

Left: Deposition *by* Paolo Veronese. Right: Two Capricci, *by* Francesco Guardi.

The Cathedral and the Baptistry

Above left: *romanesque and Gothic on the* façade *of the* Duomo*; right: the interior.* Below, left: *the interior of* San Giovanni in Fonte, *the city's* Baptistery*; right: a detail of the* baptismal font. Facing page, right: *the famous altarpiece of the* Assumption *by* Titian *(1530).*

Three works in particular stand out where the 12th century **Cathedral** and the adjoining **church of San Giovanni in Fonte**, the old **Baptistery** of the cathedral itself, are concerned – in the **Duomo**, the stupendous *Portale* and **Titian**'s altarpiece depicting the *Assumption of the Virgin*, and in the Baptistery, the splendid *baptismal font*.

The Cathedral flaunts a *façade* on which the Romanesque and Gothic both find harmonious expression. The front has a two-storeyed porch adorned with column bearing lions and reliefs – a masterpiece of Veronese Romanesque design conceived by **Maestro Niccolò** who also executed the porch on the façade of the **Basilica of San Zeno**. The *Portale* depicts two knights armed with swords fighting for Carlo Magno and flanked by saints and evangelists. Under restoration, is another Romanesque porch which depicts the adventures of *Jonah and the Whale*.

We now enter the Gothic interior with its lavish array of artistic masterpieces (**Liberale da Verona**, splendid frescoes by **Torbido** after

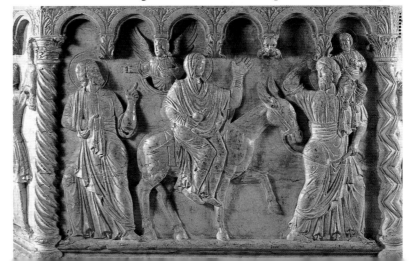

The sweet Verona of the pandoro

Who in this world has not at least once tasted Verona's traditional dessert, the sweet and soft **pandoro**? *The pandoro is now more than a hundred-years old, since a ministerial certificate and a patent was issued in 1894 to the Veronese pastry cook, Domenico Melegatti, who then had a shop in Corso Porta Borsari and who today lends his name to one of the most flourishing pastry firms which still produces the pandoro.*

The pandoro is the traditional Christmas cake of Verona. It was once called Natalino or Natalin which the Veronese derived from the Viennese tradition when the Austrians governed the city in the middle of the 19th century.

The Pandoro is made by mixing flour, milk and yeast and then left to settle before adding butter, sugar and a fresh egg. It is then baked in its distinctly-shaped mould and finally covered in a veil of icing sugar.

No Italian table is without a pandoro at Christmas and because it's so delicious it is also now eaten all year around.

cartoons by **Giulio Romano** adorning the *sanctuary*). The true masterpiece here however is an *Assumption* by **Titian**. This work, dated at around 1535, is an admirable version of the more famous Assumption by Titian in Venice's **Santa Maria dei Frari**, a work of such innovative figurative composition that it was almost refused by its commissioners.

As is well known, Veneto possesses a wealth of Titian's work and every visitor to the area would do well to see the *Annunciation* in the Duomo of Treviso and visit the birthplace of the artist himself and Pieve di Cadore.

A small door next to the Cathedral's main altar leads into the **church of San Giovanni in Fonte**, the old baptistery. The centerpiece here is undoubtedly the octagonal red marble *baptismal font*. The reliefs depict the *Life of Jesus* with the most beautiful being, perhaps, the *Exodus to Egypt* where, curiously, the Child is not held by Mary but sits on the shoulders of John. Another curiosity is the capital depicting a cat with a mouse in its mouth.

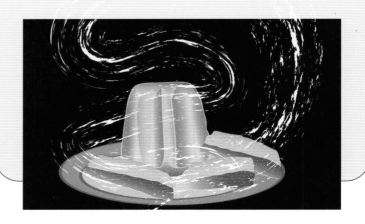

The Basilica of San
Zeno Maggiore,
*a stupendous example
of Romanesque
architecture
in Verona.*

San Zeno, pride and joy
of Veronese Romanesque

*Two of the bronze
panels of the Porch of
the* façade
of San Zeno.

Probably the most impressive religious building in Verona, the **Basilica di San Zeno Maggiore**, with its splendid pale gold tufa façade, is also among the most important examples of Romanesque architecture in the whole of Italy. Built in 1120, the Basilica was erected on the site of two previous churches, traces of which can still be seen today. The façade framed, on the one side, by the Romanesque tower and, on the other, by the red 12th century tower of the old basilica, is divided by pilaster strips and is endowed with a large circular rose window representing the *Wheel of Fortune*, constructed in the 12th century by **Maestro Brioloto**. Below, there's a large porch executed by

Maestro Niccolò in 1138 and a baldachin prothyrum supported by elegant columns and, sculpted on the architraves, the series of the months. No less impressive are the eighteen relief panels on the 12th century doors depicting scenes from the *Old* and *New Testament.*

We now enter the grandiose interior where the power of the Romanesque and the elegance of the Gothic merge to create a solemn and majestic air of spirituality, enhanced by the large cruciform pillars, the powerful arches of the columns and the high wooden Gothic ceiling. The splendor of the whole however does not distract one from noticing the two beautiful

holy-water fonts, the 12th century *baptismal font* by **Maestro Brioloto** and the 13th century stational cross.

Among the most precious works of art preserved in this basilica are without question the 12th and 13th century frescoes which recent art criticism has attributed to a First and Second **Maestro di San Zeno**. No less important is the large polychrome *statue of San Zeno* executed by **Ignoto** in the 14th century.

The pride and joy of the basilica however is the triptych over the *high altar* by **Andrea Mantegna** (around 1458) which clearly owes its inspiration to the work of Donatello. The original predella of this *Madonna and Saints*, a masterpiece of

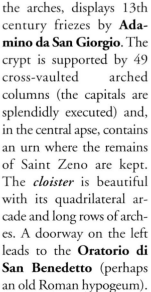

Renaissance painting in Verona, was taken off to the Louvre in Paris in Napoleonic times, meaning that the present predella is a copy. Other things to see in the basilica include a *Crucifixion* by **Altichiero** or his school and two *crucifixes*. A stairway leads to the *crypt* which, on the arches, displays 13th century friezes by **Adamino da San Giorgio**. The crypt is supported by 49 cross-vaulted arched columns (the capitals are splendidly executed) and, in the central apse, contains an urn where the remains of Saint Zeno are kept. The *cloister* is beautiful with its quadrilateral arcade and long rows of arches. A doorway on the left leads to the **Oratorio di San Benedetto** (perhaps an old Roman hypogeum).

Above, left: *the stately interior of* San Zeno*; 14th century wooden* statue of San Zeno*, preserved in the church of the same name.*
Left: *the central panel of the triptych* **Virgin with Child and Saints** *by* Andrea Mantegna.

The "hunchback" of Sant'Anastasia

A singular feature of this large old church is the presence, at the beginning of the nave, of two large holy-water fonts which are supported by two crouching human figures traditionally known as the "hunchbacks of Sant'Anastasia". The one on the right is nicknamed "Pasquino", sculpted by **Paolo Orefice**, because it was displayed for the first time in this basilica in 1591. The other, sculpted by **Gabriele Caliari**, the father of Paolo Veronese, was installed here in 1495. These two figures have the scope of inspiring charity in the rich towards all those less fortunate in the city.

Sant'Anastasia, the biggest and one of the oldest

The **Basilica di Sant'Anastasia** is the biggest and one of the most important and celebrated churches of Verona. Once upon a time two small churches stood on this site, commissioned by King Theodoric, one dedicated to Sant'Anastasia and the other to San Remigio and upheld by the Dominican order. In 1290 work was gotten underway to replace these two small churches with the basilica which stands today, dedicated to the first Dominican martyr San Pietro da Verona (however, the old name has remained). The work was to proceed for more than a century. The basilica was born thanks to the efforts of the podestà, Guglielmo di Castelbarco whose tomb, which anticipates the pensile structure of the Scaligere tombs, is to be found, if facing the basilica, on the left of the façade.

Well worth an observant gaze here is the splendid Gothic doorway among slender columns and colored marbles, enhanced by 14th century reliefs and frescoes which unfortunately have badly deteriorated. Also the two *Acquasantiere* supported by the two strange hunchbacks (see facing inset), and, in the *Sacristy*, the celebrated fresco by **Antonio Pisanello** of *Saint George and the dragon* (1433-38).

But Sant'Anastasia contains other masterpieces within its blend of Romanesque and Gothic architecture. Many paintings and sculptures are to be found within the numerous chapels lining the two naves of the basilica and the transept. In the right-hand aisle, in the third chapel, there's the *Deposition* by **Liberale da Verona**; in the fourth chapel, the *Magdalene* by the same

The Gothic splendor of Pisanello

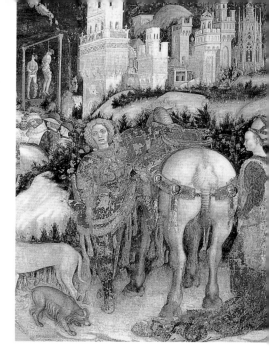

Saint George and the Princess, *painted by* Pisanello – *great 15th century painter from Pisa but who worked above all in Verona, sometimes as a court artist – is a masterpiece which recapitulates the international Gothic style of this artist, characterized by an imaginative and almost surreal sense of space where a cluster of animals, flowers and greenery painted in minute detail are pervaded by a tender and radiant light.*
Executed on the Gothic arch of the Pellegrini Chapel *between 1430 and 1440, was damaged by the gradual infiltration of rainwater over the years but was then taken down and restored and is now hung in the* Sacristy of Sant'Anastasia. *In its wash of gold and silver, this pictorial poem takes us back to the entrancing times of the late medieval.*

artist. Then there's the beautiful *St Thomas Acquinas altar* with a painting of the *Madonna with Child and Saints.*
In the transept, in the first of the five chapels from the left, we find the votive fresco depicting the *Cavalli Family Presented to the Virgin* by **Altichiero**; in the main chapel, on the right-hand wall, there's a fresco of the *Last Judgement* and the imposing funeral monument of Cortesia Serègo, as well as an *Annunciation* attributed to **Michele Giambono**.
In the left aisle, we find the almost Baroque *Rosary Chapel* with paintings by Veronese artists and, on the altar, the 14th century panel of the *Madonna del Rosario*, the protector of the city of Verona.

Above: Pisanello's *fresco in Sant'Anastasia:* Saint George and the Princess *(detail).*
Facing page, left: *the* apse, interior *and* doorway *of the church of Sant'Anastasia.*

A pause between monuments and museums

Wine and coffee: in a historical setting

Verona is the land of excellent wines and has always been lavishly endowed with osterias and wine sellers. Among the most famous is the Antica Bottega del Vino *in* Via Scudo di Francia, *a traditional meeting place for poets, writers and journalists. Here one can drink excellent "goti" and "quinte" of* Soave *and* Bardolino. *For a good cup of coffee on the other hand in an elegant place seeped in history and tradition, why not pay a visit to* Rossini *or the old* Cordioli *in* Corso Mazzini. *For a snack, besides the excellent pandoro, one might sample the* Sabbiosa cake, *a speciality of Veneto, or* Zaletti, *both of which are delicious and ideal with a glass of sweet wine.*

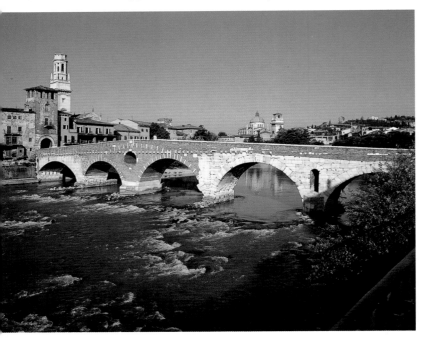

Roman Verona, the Ponte Pietra and the old theater

Left: the Roman Ponte Pietra; right: a view of the Roman theater.

A tour of Roman Verona leads one to the Adige river and its immediate surroundings where two noteworthy monuments are to be found: the **Ponte Pietra** and the **Roman Theater**, from where one can enjoy a splendid view of Verona and the elegant curve of the river. Roman Verona is completed by the precious array of artifacts gathered in the **Archaeological Museum**. The simple bridge known as Ponte Pietra is extremely elegant and was erected by the Romans (the remains of a second Roman bridge, the Postumio, can be seen near the church of Sant'Anastasia). A large part of the bridge's charm resides in the variety of materials from which it was built. The first two arches from the left date back to Roman times, the two central arches were part of a 16th century reconstruction and the last arch with the tower date back to Alberto della Scala at the end of the 1200s. Destroyed during the Second World War, the Ponte Pietra was philologically re-built with the original stones in 1957-59. And now to the Teatro Romano, which looks out over the Adige river. It lay buried until the 18th century when it was brought to light by the archaeologist **Andrea Monga**. The terraces of the cavea which are built into the hill, the stage area and the orchestra pit are all splendidly preserved. There are later buildings around the theater including the beautiful **church of Santi Siro and Libera** which dates back to the 10th century, and was then altered in the 1600s and boasts an elegant Baroque stairway. This church possesses a 14th century doorway and prothyrum and contains within notable works of art including an 18th century high altar decorated with marble tarsia and statues.

The Archaeological Museum

A wealth of artifacts enabling one to understand Roman Verona are collected in the **Museo Archeologico** *which is entered from the Roman Theater.*
Noteworthy mosaics depicting gladiator fights are on display here as well as many fine sculptures including the elegant bust of **Loricato.**
Works in bronze, statues, glass objects, urns, tombstones and mosaics are all exhibited. Among the sculpture, the Seated Female Figure *stands out, a Roman copy of a Greek original, as well as the* Statua Virile, *this too a copy of a Greek original. In the* **church of San Gerolamo,** *whose convent houses the museum, one can admire the beautiful pre-Christian floor, a 16th century* Annunciation *by* **Caroto** *and a beautiful 15th century* triptych *on the altar. The visit concludes with a trip to the* **Cloister** *from where one can enjoy another marvellous view of the city.*

Above, left: head of a satyr *and* two-faced herma. Left: Bust of Roman loricate *from the* Archaeological museum. Below: *one of its rooms.*

The celebrated inlaid woodwork of Santa Maria in Organo

Above: the celebrated inlaid woodwork of the choir (right photo) in the church of Santa Maria in Organo.
Right: the venerated wooden statue, known as the "Muleta", preserved in this church.

Inset: two views of the Giusti Gardens, among the most beautiful of late Italian Renaissance gardens.

The white marble façade of the old Olivetan church of **Santa Maria in Organo**, on the piazza of the same name, was executed by **Sanmicheli** but the real masterpiece of the church is the 15th century intarsia in colored wood which ornaments the stalls of the elegant choir and which continue on the panels of the *sacristy*. These were the work of an Olivetan monk by the name of **Fra Giovanni da Verona**. Equally impressive are the wooden *candelabrum* and the chorus' large lectern, not to mention the exceptional stall bar in the sacristy carved and inlaid by **Frà Giovanni**.

The church also contains some fine paintings in its chapels: a *Madonna and saints* by **Balestra**, the *Death of Saint John* by **G. B.**

Pittoni, a precious *Santa Francesca Romana* by **Guercino** and various frescoes by **Cavazzola** and **Brusasorci**. Two other paintings which deserve to be seen are the *Beato Bernardo Tolomei* by **Luca Giordano** and, in the left-hand aisle, **F. Morone**'s masterpiece, the *Madonna with Saints Augustine and Zeno*. The church also contains a curiosity – in a niche which is only opened on Palm Sunday, can be found the famous "Muleta". This is a rare statue in wood from the 12th century depicting Jesus riding on a mule or donkey while entering Jerusalem and is a work particularly dear to the Veronese.

The Giusti Gardens - statues, mazes and fountains

Walking down Via Carducci, one reaches Via Giardino Giusti, the 16th century Palazzo Giusti del Giardino with its monumental façade, decorated in fresco, and, above all, the famous Italian gardens which are among the most beautiful in all Italy.

The gardens are divided up into two areas: the lower area with elegant flowerbeds, mazes, fountains and statues; the other area, laid into the hill, boasts a large cypress avenue which Goethe held dear to his heart and which leads to a towered building from where one can enjoy a splendid view of the city.

A journey through history:
the impressive remains of the power of the old rulers of Verona

Castelli Scaligeri

In the area around Vicenza many testaments can still be found to the centuries in which Verona was ruled by the Della Scala family, a dynasty which begun with Mastino I in 1260 and terminated in 1387. It was Cangrande della Scala who strengthened the family's power and hastened the development of Verona and its territories. His great aspiration was to create a state which would include the whole of northern Italy. In the meantime, he set about arming and protecting the territories under his rule which ranged from the part of Garda bordering on Lombardy to the hills of Lessinia. In virtually all his jurisdictions he built formidable castles and walls until he had a network of fortifications as far as Marostica.

To take a tour of these castles, one might start by visiting the picturesque castle at Villafranca, *near Verona (16Km), then continue on to* Lonigo *(24Km) where two* Scaligero towers *survive beside the* Duomo. *One can then go to* Lazise *(22Km) to see its crenelated medieval stone and brick towers and castle. From Lazise, one can reach the* Scaligero castle in Torri del Benaco *(38Km), on the shores of Lake Garda. The beautiful town of* Sirmione, *also on Lake Garda but in Lombardy, also preserves a splendid castle, rebuilt by the Della Scalas in 1276 in order to defend themselves from attack by both sea and land. Finally, there's* Marostica *(which will be featured later in this guide) where the Scaligero family maintained two castles: the* Castello Superiore *which is now in ruins and the* Castello Inferiore.

Discovering Bardolino, Valpolicella,
Amarone, Soave and Recioto

A tour of the great Veronese wines

Between Verona and Lake Garda, lies a beautiful stretch of land which contains the most valuable vineyards in the whole of the Veneto region. Anyone interested in the art of wine making would do well to make a little tour of this area which, beginning and ending in Verona, consists of around 50km of lush vineyards and beautiful countryside. This is the zone of the great Veronese wines including the excellent light and fruity Bardolino *which is produced predominantly near Lake Garda.*
The hilly region of Monte Lessini is where the famous Valpolicella *is produced and the sweet and robust* Recioto *which is produced using a particular kind of grape dried in the open air. Another noble local wine is the* Amarone, *a high proof full-bodied red wine which also enjoys a certain fame outside Italy.* Soave, *on the other hand, is a delicate white wine.*

Two views of Lake Garda from Punta San Vigilio.

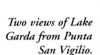

ATTRACTIONS, ENCHANTMENTS AND IMPRESSIONS OF LAKE GARDA

Around Italy's largest lake proliferate natural beauty spots, olive groves, famous vineyards, brightly-colored towns as well as regattas, sports activities and Gardaland, a paradise for children

The area immediately surrounding what is the largest lake in Italy offers the visitor a multitude of possibilities both in terms of natural landscape and historical interest, not to mention the numerous sporting activities and high level of cuisine it provides.

In the Bardolino region, for example, lay the vineyards which are famous for the fine wines they produce (see inset), while not far from Torri del Benaco sit the olive groves which are responsible for the excellent local olive oil.

Two very interesting museums can be found in the vicinity of these two areas: in Bardolino, the **Museo del vino**, at the renowned Zeni wine distillery and, in Cisano, the **Museo dell'olio di oliva** which in these parts is always of the extra virgin variety.

And on the Lombard shores, other attractions

This guide accompanies you along the banks of the part of Lake Garda which is in Veneto. But don't forget that many attractions lie on the opposite bank which lays in the province of Bergamo. Charming places like Riva del Garda, in the north or, heading south, Bogliaco, Gardone Riviera and, above all, the splendid peninsula of Sirmione, the most alluring destination of all that Lake Garda offers, are all worth a visit.

Left: *two views of the towns of* Garda *and* Bardolino.

The lake is also a great tourist attraction – so much so that the German visitors alone number more than a million every year.

Another great attraction of the lake is the sporting activities it offers, which perhaps are dominated by the famous *Centomiglia del Garda*, one of the most famous sailing races in the world. This spectacular competition which involves hundreds of boats of every size was born in 1951 on the model of the more historical car race known as the *Mille Miglia*.

Lake Garda also offers excellent shopping facilities and all the mod cons.

The small crowded resorts along the lake are lavishly strewn with elegant boutiques, artisan workshops and antique shops.

In fact you'll be surprised just what a variety and wealth of objects can be found in these resorts: from lace to dried flowers, from refined Venetian glass to the most technologically sophisticated nautical equipment and sails.

Particularly enthralling in these parts is the cuisine, based on the excellent local produce, including the wines and olive oils. The cuisine here takes its lead from various schools, depending on which part of the lake you eat, the Veneto shore or the Lombard shore.

The vibrant open air cafés on the piazzas, the walks through olive groves and vineyards, the windsurfers and bright sails on the water, the wind, the limpid skies, all make of Lake Garda one of the most desirable and popular resorts in the whole of Europe.

Poets and writers composed on these banks

The great Latin poets **Virgil** and **Catulus** came to write on the banks of Lake Garda where the latter owned a splendid villa. But above all, its contemporary writers who have enjoyed the unique spell of the area. **Goethe** was here during his Italian tour as was **Ugo Foscolo** at the beginning of the 1800s. In more recent times writers like **Marcel Proust**, **Rainer Maria Rilke**, **James Joyce** and **Ezra Pound** have all succumbed to the bewitchment of Garda.

At lunch by the lake
Splendid food from both the soil and water

Because the lake incorporates various provinces, from Brescia to Verona, so too does the cuisine vary from place to place. Here follows a list of dishes you might expect to find served in the restaurants of the area. Firstly, there's **polenta con gli osei** *(polenta with fried game);* **asparagus** *is especially popular around the Vicenza and Treviso areas of the lake as are white and black* **truffles** *which are grown in the area. A famous dish here is* **tortellini al sedano** *and the* **gnocchi** *known locally as* **caponesi**. *Chicory is famous throughout the region and used in many dishes. But perhaps the most popular food of all along the banks of the lake is, not surprisingly fish from the lake itself. Dishes include,* **trout fillets** *in local oil,* **perch fillets**, **baked tench**, **fried bleak**, **boiled eels**, *the delicious* **carp** *and* **whitefish** *baked in foil.*

Among the olive groves of Monte Baldo, the vineyards of Bardolino, the Castle of Malcesine and the enchantment of Lake Garda

Panorama of the town of Malcesine. *Below:* Lake Garda is often the venue of sporting events

Wolfgang Goethe took the time to stop off in **Malcesine** during his famous tour of Italy. Today, tourists have the added luxury of being able to take a cablecar to the top of **Monte Baldo** which, at 2,000 meters, commands a stunning view of the surroundings.

In the vicinity there are also a number of nature reserves including the **Riserva della Gardesana Orientale**. Malcesine is situated in a splendid natural setting and has a charm of its own thanks to its medieval streets, its castle and the vibrancy typical of every fishing center. Small narrow alleys wind through the thickly stacked houses and eventually lead down to the lake. Of special interest is the old crenelated **Palazzo dei Capitani del Lago**. Continuing along the shore of the lake one then arrives in **Garda**, with its swarm of lively cafés and the old Palazzo dei Capitani which dates back to the 1400s and was the work of the Venetians. Garda also has a small town museum. From Garda one soon arrives in **Bardolino** which is important for various reasons, one of which is its antiquity as it was a lake dwelling in prehistoric times and later a Roman settlement. Among the medieval remains still to be seen there's the crenelated tower in Piazza Matteoti. Worth a visit is the **Chiesa di San Zeno** of Carolingian origin. But Bardolino is important above all as the production center of the excellent wines which originate from the fine vineyards extending from Verona down to Lake Garda.

Lazise

Torri del Benaco

A medieval fortified wall encloses the historical center of **Lazise**. The towered 14th century castle is part of the park of the **Villa Bernini Buri**.

As is the case with many of these lakeside towns, the small harbor is particularly pretty and the chief monuments are to be found in this vicinity like the small Romanesque **Chiesa di San Niccolò** and the 16th century customs warehouse known as the **Dogana Vecchia**.

Lazise is today the principle port of the eastern shore of Lake Garda.

Lazise also features in the Wine Tour (see inset on facing page) and offers fine products from the nearby vines.

This pretty town sits at the foot of Monte Baldo and is at the center of the Riviera degli Ulivi. The castle with its three crenelated towers dates back to 1383 and now houses the **Museo Civico** where, alongside the archaeological exhibits on display, you'll also find the instruments and tools traditionally used for the cultivation of the olive groves. The most interesting monuments of this pretty town which huddles around its picturesque harbor include the beautiful **Chiesa della SS. Trinità** and the 18th century **Chiesa dei santi Pietro e Paolo**. Here too stands the massive fortification which dates back to the 11th century and is known as the **Torre di Berengario**. This town is also the starting point for crossing the stunning Riviera degli Ulivi, a lush virgin world of olive groves whose shimmering green tones are off-set by the dazzling blues of the lake.

Left: Lazise *and,* right, *a panorama of* Torri del Benaco, *at the heart of the* Riviera degli Ulivi.

In the fantastic city of Gardaland

Created in 1975 and growing larger by the year – it now covers 700,000 square meters – Gardaland is the largest theme park in Italy and can be found very close to Peschiera. Here, everything is geared to keeping the children happy – from the reconstruction of the Egyptian temple of Abu Simbel to the dolphin aquarium called Palablu which provides a valuable insight into marine biology.

There's also a huge Planetarium which is in fact the largest in Europe and the many special events that Gardaland puts on, like the medieval tournament which is held in the nearby Merlin's Castle or the acrobats and clowns and mime artists who perform in the vicinity of the pirate ship. There's also the charming little steam train, the Trans Gardaland Express, the rides along the river in canoes made of a tree-trunk to the accompaniment of African drums beating in the surrounding "jungle" and the Wild West city of Rio Brown. In short, the perfect day out for the kids.

Veneto cuisine: recipes

Baccalà (Codfish)

BACCALÀ MANTECATO. Immerse the cod in a saucepan full of cold water and bring to the boil. Leave cod to dry for about twenty minutes. Press the cod and from time to time add olive oil until the fish has absorbed it. Serve when cool with a little garlic, parsley, a little salt and pepper and polenta.

INGREDIENTS (SERVES FOUR). 800 grams of cod; garlic; olive oil; parsley; salt and pepper.

SALT COD STEWED WITH MILK AND ONIONS (BACCALÀ ALLA VICENTINA). (This is one of the most famous of all Veneto specialities and is prepared in a variety of different ways.) Without removing the skin, debone the cod and then cut into largish slices. Cover with flour and place in a frying pan. Garnish with a little salt, pepper, cinnamon and parmesan cheese. In another pan, sauté an onion and some garlic in a little olive oil. Add two anchovies and soak in a quarter of a liter of white wine. When the wine has been absorbed pour in half a liter of milk. Complete the sauce with a knob of butter and then pour over the sliced cod in the other pan, covering it. Place in the oven and cook until the sauce is reduced.

INGREDIENTS (SERVES FOUR). 800 grams of salted codfish; flour; salt; pepper; cinnamon; parmesan cheese; olive oil; onion; garlic; anchovies; parsley; white wine; milk and butter.

CODFISH ALLA TREVISANA (BACCALÀ ALLA TREVISANA). Remove the scales and bones from the fish and cut into large pieces. Slice an onion and sauté half in an earthenware pot with a little oil. Place over the onion a layer of cod slices covered in flour, on top of which arrange the other half of the onion. Add salt, pepper, a little nutmeg and more olive oil. Sauté for ten minutes. Soak in wine until it's absorbed. Continue cooking for a further two hours, adding slowly a liter of milk. Place the fish on a layer of grated parmesan cheese and parsley. Add a few more tablespoons of olive oil and place in an oven. Cook for another half an hour.

INGREDIENTS (SERVES FOUR). One and a half kg of cod; 500 grams of onion; olive oil; salt; pepper; nutmeg; one glass of white wine; one liter of milk; 100 grams of parmesan cheese and parsley.

Veneto cuisine: recipes

Polenta

POLENTA AND GAME (POLENTA ED OS-EI). *This is one of the most typical dishes in Veneto, especially in the mountainous regions. Clean and wash the game. Boil a large saucepan of water with a liter and half of salted water. Add the corn flour and stir often. When it comes to the boil turn down the flame and let the polenta simmer for three quarters of an hour. In the meantime, place the game in a pan with a sliced onion, sliced bacon, olive oil, butter and sage leaves. When half cooked pour in some red wine and cook for another twenty minutes. When the polenta is cooked pour it onto a plate, forming a hollow at the center where the game is placed and then serve.*

INGREDIENTS (SERVES FOUR). 400 grams of corn flour; 20 small birds; 100 grams of bacon; one onion; one glass of red wine; sage; butter; olive oil and salt.

POLENTA RISSOLES (POLPETE DE PO-LENTA). *This is a very old recipe dating back to the nineteenth century. Prepare a soft polenta and garnish with butter and grated parmesan cheese. Prepare separately a sauce of chicken giblets, minced meat, tomato sauce, salt and olive oil. Mix with the polenta. When cooled, slice the polenta into rissoles and place in an oven for a few minutes. Cover the rissoles in breadcrumbs and fry in boiling oil. Serve piping hot.*

INGREDIENTS (SERVES FOUR). 350 grams of corn flour; 50 grams of butter; 100 grams of parmesan cheese; 300 grams of chicken giblets; 200 grams of minced beef; 30 grams of olive oil; 200 grams of besciamella sauce; breadcrumbs; tomato sauce and salt.

BAKED SAUSAGE AND LARD POLENTA (SMACAFAM). *This is an old mountain recipe which involves white flour rather than corn flour like most polenta. Stir the white flour into a broth and add salt and pepper. Slice up the sausages and fry together with some lard cut up into cubes. Stir the sausages into the broth and pour into a greased baking dish. Garnish with a few more slices of sausage and cook in the oven at a high temperature for an hour.*

INGREDIENTS (SERVES FOUR PEOPLE). 300 grams of white flour; 200 grams of sausages; 80 grams of lard; 1 3/4 liter of broth; salt and pepper.

BELLUNO

Small, elegant and situated high above the confluence of the Ardo with the Piave, this tranquil city with its Veneto Renaissance colors and lively promenades is full of charm.

A tour of Belluno should begin from Piazza dei Martiri, which, with its overriding Renaissance character, is the social hub of the city thanks to the famous promenade beneath the arches on the north side of the piazza known as the *liston*. The piazza is also graced with gardens and a fountain. Here one should certainly pay a visit to the **Chiesa di San Rocco** and

Above: Palazzo dei Rettori, *one of the most beautiful palaces in Belluno which is now the* Prefecture.

Chamois and roe deer salami and smoked ricotta cheese

Belluno is all valleys, mountains, shrouded peaks, natural springs and limpid fish-infested torrents. The natural, healthy character of the area is reflected in the simple wholesome culinary fare favored by the local population. Every val-ley boasts its specialities, among which you'll find dishes such as fongadina, patugoi, sciosi *and* bisati *and all of which are well worth sampling. Chamois and* roe deer salamis *are a local speciality, as are* smoked ricotta cheese *and another cheese known as* malga. *As for fruit,* raspberries, blackberries *and* strawberries *are all grown* in the surrounding countryside. A dish for those with a healthy appetite is the zuppa di fagioli alla bellunese – a dense broth consisting of pieces of pork, white beans and pasta.

It also goes without saying that polenta is a staple part of the diet in the area as is more or less the case throughout the Veneto region.

Left: *a panoramic view of Belluno with, in the background,* Monte Serva. Center: *the picturesque* Piazza delle Erbe. Below, left: *the* church of Santo Stefano *with its impressive doorway.* Below, right: Porta Dojona.

its many 16th century paintings. The city essentially revolves around Via Mezzaterra which is surrounded by colonnaded little streets and small squares, the most picturesque being perhaps the 15th century Piazza delle Erbe. The city flaunts a host of different architectural styles – so that a distinctly medieval feel will suddenly give way to a taste of the Venice of the fifthteenth and

sixteenth centuries which finds expression in some truly stunning palaces. At either end of Via Mezzaterra stand the city's two principal gates – at the northern end, the medieval **porta Dojona** and at the southern end **porta Rugo**. The principle monuments of Belluno date back to the 15th and 16th centuries and thus belong to the high Gothic and Renaissance

The rebirth of Longarone, home of ice cream

This small town in the Piave valley is famous for a tragedy which occurred in 1963 when an avalanche, destroying the dam of Vaiont, caused a huge flood. Raging waters, clogged with mud, swept through the small town of Longarone, causing such devastation and damage that the town had to be completely re-built.

Among other things Longarone is known for its ice cream and every year a large festival is held here, attracting artisans of the trade from all over Europe.

Piazza del Duomo,
*the social hub
for the inhabitants
of Belluno.*

periods. The Gothic **church of Santo Stefano** is well worth visiting with its beautiful interior and impressive *cloister*.

A necessary port of call for any visitor to Belluno is the **Duomo**. It was built by **Tullio Lombardo** in the 16th century and contains valuable works of art by artists such as Schiavone, Jacopo Bassano, Palma il Giovane and Sebastiano Ricci. Another church worth a visit for the paintings it contains is the **Chiesa di Santa Maria di Lore-** **to**. Belluno though also possesses some fine civic architectural achievements, not least of which is the **Palazzo dei Rettori**, a fine example of Venetian Renaissance architecture which can be found near the Duomo. The **Torre Civica** is impressive as are the **Palazzo Piloni** which contains frescoes by the 16th century artist Cesare Vecellio and **Palazzo dei Giuristi**, now the civic museum, where paintings by Palma il Giovane and Luca Giordano can be found among many others. The theater is neoclassical, built in the 19th century.

Ten itineraries taking in the villas of the Belluno region

With the approval of the European Union, ten cultural itineraries have been established in the Belluno region which include visits to a series of villas on the outskirts of the city. These are not the stately Palladian villas of the Vicenza region but rather excellent examples of the creation of a harmony between the environment and architecture, between the life unfolding in the villa and the work in the fields. Some of these villas can be found near the Bellunesi Nature Reserve. *The ones which deserve a special mention include* Villa Pasole, Villa Alpago Novello (photo right), Villa Morazzuti, Villa Sandi-Zaso, Villa Buzzati (photo above) *and* Villa Fauro Centenere.

The old artisan traditions of working with wood and iron are still thriving today. Once upon a time the swords produced in Belluno were famous throughout the world

A reporter once wrote: "Belluno was once made famous by the exquisite wealth of swords and other weapons produced by its artisans who, to this day, continue to turn out masterful examples of their craft." In fact, during the period between the 15th and 17th centuries, the swords produced in Belluno enjoyed a worldwide fame and were exported to many nations including even those in the East. It is even said that the swords used by the Scottish warriors bore the hallmark of **Andrea Ferrara**, a famous maker of arms of the period. He was a craftsman who became famous, above all, for a sword known as the *Schiavona*. However, Belluno is also renowned for its fine tradition in carpentry and stone working.

Left: *images of Belluno's thriving artisan tradition.* Below: *the "zater of the Piave" who sail their rafts from the mountains to the sea.*

Raftsmen on the Piave

A trip along the historic river Piave would be a splendid way of becoming acquainted with the area and would confront the passenger with many places of exceptional beauty and rich in tradition.
Codissago, in the commune of Castellavazzo, is the center which keeps alive the memory of a great tradition: that of the raftsmen of the Piave, *strong ruddy men who sailed large rafts along the river, linking for centuries the Belluno area with Venice to where they carried wood and other local produce. Often they would tow along behind them huge tree trunks which must have made for a spectacular sight.*
Other points of interest along the river include Ponte delle Alpi *with its historical bridge which is almost a thousand years old,* Sospirolo *with the stupendous* Charterhouse of Vedana, Sedico *with its beautiful villas, including* Villa Miari, Lentiai *and* Mel, *an old Roman settlement where the only surviving medieval castle in the Belluno region can be found,* Castello di Zumelle.

Feltre's Piazza Maggiore.

A city of illustrious personalities

Feltre boasts a great cultural tradition, is endowed with a fine university and was the home of many illustrious personalities. **Vittorino dei Rambaldoni** was from Feltre, a great humanist and pedagogue who founded a school which succeeded in providing a marvellous education in the ideals and values of the Renaissance. Feltre was also the birthplace of **Panfilo Castaldi**, doctor and printer who lived in the 15th century and at Gutenberg won a prize for inventing movable type.
It was in Feltre, in the beautiful theater of the Palazzo dei Rettori, that the great Venetian playwright **Carlo Goldoni** was said to have staged his early comedies in 1738. The loggia of this palazzo carries the signature of another great Veneto artist, **Andrea Palladio** who of course was to exert such a profound influence on both European and American architecture in the following centuries.

Feltre

In the province of Belluno, this old walled city in the middle of a mountain basin, has much to offer in the way of beauty and culture, from its frescoed façades, its tradition in wrought iron to its historical Palio

Feltre is probably one of the most interesting walled cities in the Veneto. It was completely re-built by the Venetians in the 16th century when they took it under their wing after it had been razed to the ground by the preceding wars. Feltre, in common with many of the towns in the region, is distinguished by the liveliness and grace of its squares. Starting from Campo San Giorgio, a square animated by a market, which is flanked by the city walls on one side, we encounter the splendid 16th century **Porta Imperiale**. We then arrive in Piazzetta Trento e Trieste where the beautiful **Palazzo Crico-Tauro** with its frescoes by Lorenzo Luzzo can be found. The main thoroughfare of the city is Via Mezzaterra which is lined with frescoed palaces. Here can be found the **church of San Giacomo** with its neoclassical interior and immediately afterwards a series of interesting buildings such as **Palazzo Bellati Villabruna** with its painted ceilings in the style of Sansovino and its beautiful entrance hall which leads to a hanging garden and stables. One's attention is then attracted upwards towards

Palazzo Salce Aldovini Mezzanotte whose façade is decorated with frescoes of scenes from ancient Rome.

Feltre almost resembles an open-air museum as a result of all its frescoed palaces, like **Palazzo Facen Orum dall'Armi** and **Palazzo Cantoni** which stands out thanks to its elegant frescoes. Our walk through Feltre now leads us to the peace and quiet of Piazza Maggiore which is laid out on many levels and with its arches, steps, churches and fountain evokes a mesmerizing effect. Here can be found **Palazzo della Ragione** with its Palladian portico and **Palazzo Pretorio**, now the town hall, where once the Venice Government would sit and where, in the chancellery, the great 18th century playwright Carlo Goldoni worked. The *Sala degli Stemmi* inside the palazzo is graced by elegantly painted wooden beams. At the southern end of the piazza we come across two more stately palaces, **Palazzo Romagno** and **Palazzo Bovio**; to the north, on the other hand, stands the **castle** and the **church of Santi Rocco e Sebastiano**. Presiding over the piazza we find the *Lion of San Marco*, paying testament to the power once held by the Venetian Republic and two *statues* of two of Feltre's famous native sons, the pedagogue *Vittorino da Feltre* and the master typographer, *Panfilo Castaldi*.

Towards Piazzetta della Legna, stands **Palazzo Guarnieri**, a 16th century building which for centuries was the home of the Monte di Pietà, or pawnbrokers, and still today conserves the stalls where this lively and important business was carried out. Not far from here, we encounter Via Paradiso which is where the **Galleria d'Arte Carlo Rizzarda** is located, a very interesting museum that is discussed in more detail below. We now reach Largo de' Mizzan, home of **Palazzo Mizzan** which is adorned by an interesting cycle of frescoes.

Palazzo Villabruna is the home of the **Museo Civico**, a museum full of interesting exhibits including a *Christ with Saints Peter and Paul* by **Cima da Conegliano**, *a Resurrection of Lazarus* by **Palma il Vecchio**, beautiful landscape paintings by Marco Ricci and a small portrait by **Gentile Bellini**. The museum is also endowed with an interesting archaeological section, including bronzes, statues and memorial tablets from the Roman period as well as coins, ceramics and objects in gold. It also contains a reconstruction of the living conditions of a typical noble family in the 18th century.

We now pass beyond the walls of the city and encounter Feltre's **Duomo**. The **Cathedral of San Pietro** contains the 16th century *tomb of Andrea Bellati* by **Tullio Lombardo**. The

Santuario dei santi Vittore e Corona

A local place of veneration, this church near Monte Miesna was founded as far back as 1096 and soon afterwards built in a Byzantine-Romanesque style. The three-aisled interior and beautiful **cloister** are decorated with frescoes executed by notable artists. The **chapels** lining Via Crucis which leads up to the church were built in the 17th century.

A Museum of wrought iron

Something of a curiosity in Feltre is the Galleria d'Arte Moderna Carlo Rizzarda *which is located in Via Paradiso.* Carlo Rizzarda (1883-1931) *was an artist who worked with wrought iron and the museum was founded to conserve his work and the work of other artists in the same field. Working with wrought iron is an art which is still practiced today in many parts of the Veneto region, like Conegliano, Verona and Vittorio Veneto. In Mogliano, near Treviso, there's an international academy of iron which attracts masters of the art and students from all over the world. The Galleria Rizzarda also houses many Italian paintings from the 19th and 20th centuries, including works by Giovanni Fattori, Telemaco Signorini, Carlo Carrà and Felice Casorati.*

The Palio of Feltre

During the first week of every August the splendid Palio *takes place in Feltre in which the four districts of the city take part. The procession of the participants and the flag bearers is in itself an impressive spectacle but it's the horse race at the end of the day between representatives of the four districts which provides the real excitement. The winner receives the Palio which every year is designed by a different artist. Every district holds supper parties out in the open at the end of the week's festivities and the entire city participates. The Palio commemorates an important event in the history of Feltre – the admission of the city into the Venetian Republic which took place on June 15, 1404.*

Baptistery is also interesting with an old *baptismal font* of 1339. One cannot leave Feltre without also having visited in the 16th century **Palazzo Cumano** the **Galleria d'Arte Moderna**. This modern art gallery contains work by fine artists of the late 19th and 20th centuries such as Signorini, Previati, Induno, Fattori, Tosi, Cascella, Carrà, Casorati and Maccari.

Finally, having perhaps enjoyed a meal in one of Feltre's fine restaurants (mushrooms, beans, nuts and grappa are among the local specialities), one would do well to take an excursion up to the **Santuario di San Vittore e Corona** (see inset on adjacent page).

Pedavena, home of beer

Three kilometers from Feltre, lies Pedavena, *known locally as the queen of beer. It's also the locality of one of the area's most impressive villas, the 17th century* Villa Pasole *which sits at the foot of the mountains. But the main attraction of Pedavena is unquestionably the historic beer factory known as the* Birreria *and in operation since the end of the 19th century. The 20th century artist Walter Resenterra painted frescoes of legends of the Dolomites in its winter garden and the building as a whole with its columns and stairways and copper counters is full of character.*

The Dolomiti Bellunesi Nature Reserve

Thirty two thousand hectares of stunning landscapes: alpine peaks more than two thousand meters high, one thousand five hundred different species of flora and a rare wildlife including mouflon (wild sheep) and golden eagles as well as the remains of a man who lived twelve thousand years ago

This recently established National Park occupies 32,000 hectares of mountainous terrain. The park as a whole provides a wealth of contrasts; gorges, meadows, forests and sheer vertical walls all combine to create a stunning natural environment which is further enriched by its huge variety of flora. The park incorporates the outer ramifications of the Dolomites, including the **Alpi Feltrine** with **Mount Pavione** (2335m). This stunning setting where the melting glaciers have created depressions and caverns almost a thousand meters deep, also contains almost 1,500 rare species of flora including the alpine delphinium and the sempervivum of the Dolomites. Though bears, wolves and lynx have now vanished from the area there still remains a vast number of chamois deer, roe-deer and mouflon. The white partridge, black grouse and the royal eagle are among the among the birds to be found in the park. Often the landscapes evoke a sense of eternity and almost one can imagine a world in which prehistoric man had his existence; in fact, the remains of a man more than twelve thousand years old were found in Val Rosta not so long ago.

The history of man's working relationship with the mountains is preserved in the shepherds' huts on the slopes and the *pendane*, old animal shelters which are to be found along the mule tracks. The park also contains an architectural jewel, the old **Charterhouse of Vedàna**, a testament to the faith of the local population.

Above, left: *the Val di Piero.* Above, right: *an inlet of* Lake del Mis *in the* Dolomiti Bellunesi Nature Reserve. Below, left: *a chamois deer in the snow.* Below, right: *the splendid* Certosa di Vedàna.

Vittorio Veneto, *founded in the 1800s, is an elegant and austere town, pervaded by memories of the First World War*

A stunning panorama of Vittorio Veneto.

The origins of this town which was created in name in the middle of the 19th century came about when two very old communities, Ceneda and Serravalle decided to merge and form one community. Ceneda was to the north and isolated among the mountains while Serravalle was to the south, near the shores of the Meschio; the station and town hall which served both communities was located half way between the two towns. Later, Vittorio Veneto was to become famous for the victory won there over the Austrians which put an end to the First World War (1918).

Before entering the town, one encounters the **church of Santa Giustina** which contains the *Tomb of Rizzardo da Camino* (1335) whose sarcophagus is mounted by impressive statues. The **Duomo** contains **Titian**'s *Madonna with Child and SS Andrew and Peter*. There are also paintings by Francesco da Milano in the *choir*. The political power of the town is represented by the beautiful **Palazzo della Comunità**, or **Loggia di Serravalle**, a 15th century arcaded building with faded frescoes on its façade. It now houses the interesting **Museo del territorio cenedese** which contains a section dedicated to Roman antiquities as well as valuable works of art including a *Madonna with Child* by **Sansovino**. Near the 14th century hospital stands the small **church of San Lorenzo**. We now enter the Ceneda district and immediately encounter the old **Castello di San Martino** which is now the seat of the Bishop of Vittorio Veneto and then the main piazza where the beautiful 18th century **Duomo** and the elegant **Loggia del Sansovino** can be found.

At the table: polenta and game and Merlot wine

It's a treat eating in these parts. Besides the traditional polenta and game (known as osei), local specialities include roe deer and polenta, kid cooked on a spit, guinea-fowl and trout cooked in white wine. All the traditional cheeses of the Veneto region are on offer here as well as the extremely tasty cao de lat, *which is a kind of mascarpone cheese. Other specialities include dry meats, bacon and, when in season, mushrooms and strawberries. The area is also renowned for its large selection of high quality wines such as* Raboso, Cabernet, Merlot, *and the* Torchiato of Vittorio Veneto.

Veneto cuisine: recipes

Desserts

FRITTER (FRITOLE). *This very popular form of pancake can also be made with apples and rice but here we propose the recipe using wheat flour. Place the flour in a bowl and stir in yeast after it's been soaked in warm water. Add vanilla sugar, a little salt, grated lemon peel, a touch of cinnamon, candied citron, pine nuts and raisins soaked in rum. Stir with a wooden spoon and let sit for four hours in a covered bowl. Stir the mixture, adding a liter water or milk. Fry some oil in a frying pan and add tablespoons of the mixture. Drain the fritters on absorbent paper and sprinkle icing sugar over them.*

INGREDIENTS. 500 grams of flour; 50 grams of vanilla sugar; 100 grams of raisins; 50 grams of pine nuts; 50 grams of candied citron; 40 grams of brewer's yeast; lemon; rum; cinnamon; olive oil; icing sugar and salt.

FUGAZZA DI PASQUA. *This is a typical Easter cake. Place 250 grams of wheat flour in a bowl with a little salt and 75 grams of yeast which has been softened in warm milk. Stir the mixture until it becomes soft. Leave to rise for about an hour. Then stir again the mixture and add three beaten eggs, 300 grams of sugar, another 300 grams of flour and some butter. Again stir the mixture until it becomes soft and leave*

to sit for another two hours. Add three more egg yolks, the remaining flour and some more butter. Leave to sit for another five hours. Stir the mixture again and then form into three flat cakes, brushing the top with egg yolk. Cook in the oven at a moderate heat for forty minutes.*

INGREDIENTS. 1250 grams of wheat flour; 300 grams of sugar; 7 eggs; 75 grams of brewer's yeast; milk; butter and salt.

APPLE STRUDEL (STRUDEL DE POMI). *Mix the flour with sugar, salt, eggs and butter and stir into hot water. Leave to sit for twenty minutes. Peel the apples and cut into smallish slices and together with the sugar, raisins, grappa, pine nuts, cinnamon, lemon peel and breadcrumbs browned in butter place on the layer of pastry. Roll the pastry over the filing, place in a greased oven dish and cook at 250° for fifty minutes. Serve with a sprinkling of icing sugar.*

INGREDIENTS. 270 grams of wheat flour; 20 grams of sugar; 50 grams of butter; 1 kg of apples; 60 grams of breadcrumbs; 50 grams of butter for the filling; 50 grams of sugar for the filling; 60 grams of pine nuts and raisins for the filling; cinnamon and lemon peel.

A splendid view of Alleghe (photo by R. Ghedina).

THE DOLOMITES,
LEGENDARY MOUNTAINS

Exceptional natural beauty, mountain peaks, lakes, snow, meadows and woods as well as winter sports

Stratifications of sedimentary origin consisting of dolomite and calcite, the Dolomites are an impressive array of towering rocks, eerie pinnacles and lush forests and meadows which rise to great heights – Marmolada (3354 meters), Civetta (3218 meters) and Tofane (3243 meters) – and are also graced by dazzling ravines, waterfalls and many splendid lakes.

One of the great merits of the Dolomites is their accessibility. A great number of trails and walks exist by which one can enter into the secret heart of this splendid natural environment. Fauna are plentiful throughout the Dolomite region and an especially large number of birds, including eagles, falcons and more than sixty different types of songbird.

For lovers of a more worldly environment, **Cortina**, both during the summer and winter, is a lively center of cultural initiatives. There are also many ethnographic and palaeontological museums in the area. There's also the possibility of experiencing some of the traditional customs and folklore of the region in the form of the alpine choirs and

The lake of Auronzo *near* Cortina d'Ampezzo *(photo by R. Ghedina).*

bands, the mountain carnivals and the crafts of the local artisans. In the summer there's a park which is easily accessible and graced with forests, lakes, waterfalls where one can also hire a canoe or fish. All manner of wildlife can be observed here in its natural habitat, including deer, chamois, ermines and marmots. There are now also bears and lynx.

During the winter, the region offers ample opportunities for all kinds of winter sports – skiing, snow-boarding, sledding, including both motor-sleds and dog drawn sleds.

At the heart of the Dolomites, there are many resorts from which to choose: **Agordo**, a tourist center with a long tradition; the district of the **Civetta** peak which incorporates the locality of **Alleghe**. Alternatively, there are places like **Rocca Pietore** or **Malga Ciapela** that lead up to the ascent of the **Marmolada**, the highest mountain in the Dolomite range which stands an impressive 3270 meters high.

SPORT AND RECREATION FOR EVERY SEASON

The Dolomites are in a position to offer a wide range of sports and leisure activities throughout the year. In the winter, all the ski *resorts bustle with activity where ski touring is another option. Many sled rides are also provided including those* drawn *by horses as well as* snow-boarding *and excursions into the uncontaminated depths of this natural wonderland. During springtime, when the meadows begin to replenish their lush green carpets, nature lovers are able to amuse themselves for hours on end as the exquisite wealth of flora comes into flower and the region's wildlife emerge from their winter retreats. In the summer one can* fish *and* canoe *on the lakes in the midst of breathtaking landscapes. Other sporting facilities offered by the area enable one to enjoy pastimes such as* archery, golf, surfing *and* horse riding.

The local artisans also lend great character to the mountain villages and towns and the restaurants of the region offer the local specialities which we've already discussed in this guide.

Cadore, among lakes and mountain peaks

Nature, art and culture around Pieve di Cadore and other places of incomparable beauty

A curiosity: the museum of spectacles

The entire history of an appendage which has greatly benefited the human race: *spectacles*. Four centuries covering the history of this simple but ingenious aid to the human eye including sunglasses which began their existence as far back as the 18th century. This museum, in the province of Pieve di Cadore, reveals everything you might want to know about the history of spectacles.

Above, left: the Dolomites of Cortina and the Tre Cime di Lavaredo *(photo by R. Ghedina).* Below, right: *the house where Titian was born.*

The vast area around Cadore, rich in art and culture, extends from Marmarole to Pelmo al Cridola. The historical capital of this area is **Pieve di Cadore**, famous in artistic circles because it was here, in 1477, that **Tiziano Vecellio**, or **Titian**, as he's known as in English-speaking countries, was born. One can visit the house where the great artist was born in Pieve di Cadore. In **Tai di Cadore**, on the other hand, there's a rather curious museum, the **Museo dell'Occhiale**, dedicated to the history of spectacles (see column on left). There are also other intriguing points of interest in the vicinity of Pieve di Cadore: skirting the lake, one encounters **Domegge**, **Lozzo** and **Calalzo** where, among other things, are to be found the famous **Fonti di Lagole** – hot springs of ferruginous water. In the Oltrepiave region, **Vigo di Cadore** is graced by several old churches, among which are **Sant'Orsola** and **Santa Margherita di Salagona**. Finally, on the lake of Santa Caterina there's **Auronzo di Cadore** with the beautiful **Misurina** and the **Tre Cime di Lavaredo**, a celebrated ski station.

SUMMER AND WINTER RESORTS

The vast region known as the **Cadorina** *which stretches from* **Marmarole** *to* **Pelmo al Cridola**, *has as its capital* **Pieve di Cadore**, *famous for the fact that* Titian, *the great Venetian artist, was born here. Not far away can be found* **Domegge**, **Lozzo** *and* Calalzo, *the first railway stop on the Dolomite line and famous for its hot springs.*
Pope John Paul II spent his vacations in **Vigo** *and* **Lorenzago di Cadore**. *Other places worth visiting in the area include* **Auronzo** *(on the* lake *of Santa Caterina),* **Misurina** *(with the three summits of* Lavaredo), **Comelico Superiore**, **Santo Stefano di Cadore**, **Selva di Cadore**, **Agordo** *and* **Forno di Zoldo**, *all of which possess winter sports facilities.*

Cortina, queen of the Dolomites

Italian salon of the Alps, crowned by legendary peaks, and an international tourist and sporting center

Set in the glorious frame provided by the peaks of the **Tofane** and the **Cristallo**, **Cortina** sits at an altitude of 1224 meters and is reached by means of various mountain passes like the **Tre Croci,** the **Falzarego** and the **Giau**. Cortina is one of the most celebrated tourist and sports centers in the whole of Europe: it is known as the queen of the Dolomites and salon of the Alps and has much to offer the visitor. During the summer, when the mountains glow pink, one can enjoy its trails and walks (there are, in fact, almost 300 kilome-

ters of paths). The sporting facilities are, as you would expect, excellent: tennis, golf, horse riding, swimming and skiing are all splendidly catered for. In the winter Cortina boasts a 110 kilometers of cross-country ski runs and 58 ski slopes served by 37 ski lifts. Those who do not ski can ice skate, go sledding or rock climb. The hotels and restaurants of Cortina are renowned for their comfort and quality. The town also possesses a thriving shopping center and a lively initiative where the arts are concerned.

The imposing mountain of Gusela. Above, left: Cortina d'Ampezzo *under the snow (photo by R. Ghedina).*

LOCAL CUISINE IN CORTINA'S FAMOUS RESTAURANTS

Cortina has a rich and interesting culinary tradition. Many of its first courses rely heavily on locally grown produce, like turnips, potatoes, herbs *and* cheeses.
Polenta is a great favorite of the area as are mushrooms *both served up in an infinite variety of ways.*
The game of the Dolomites often provides a hearty main course. Local desserts include "strudel", "krapfen" and the delicious crostate, *a tart filled with blackcurrants, ricotta cheese, apples and pine nuts.*

Right: *the* Canale dei Buranelli; far right: *a view of* Piazza Signori *with the 14th century* palazzo. Below: *the* Sile *at* Ponte Vecchio.

Wonders bearing the stamp of Treviso

Appropriately, the vast stunning area which makes up the trevigiano territory has been defined "la Marca felice" (the happy march) – a title referring to the old medieval administrative and political district. In fact, the high quality of life in this region is maintained by an abundance of different factors – the natural beauty of the environment with its mountains, hills and plains being perhaps the principle benefit enjoyed by the local population. The history of the region is well preserved with splendid collections of Roman antiquities, old walled towns, castles and, above all, a wealth of stupendous villas in the great Veneto tradition. Great artists like Giorgione, Titian, Cima da Conegliano and Canova are all well represented in the region by works of stupendous artistic merit. Finally, the relaxed and friendly nature of the local people manifests itself in the fine cuisine of the area, many of whose great variety of dishes originate from the kitchens of the *contadini*. The wines of the area are also of exceptionally high quality and the many vineyards of the region lend a picturesque quality to the landscapes of the Treviso area.

TREVISO

Beautiful landscapes, buildings seeped in history, a fervent entrepreneurial prowess and a culinary expertise combine to create the spirit of this elegant and gentle city known as Treviso.

Treviso is a beautiful, lively city where history, nature and vitality all find expression. Though a peaceful and elegant city it is also blessed with a driving entrepreneurial spirit which has kept unemployment in the area down to a bare minimum and manifests itself in the flourishing export business the city enjoys. Time and nature have been kind to Treviso, blessing the city with an extraordinary wealth of natural springs and picturesque canals which have inspired Treviso's nickname as the "little Venice". The beautiful Canale dei Buranelli is especially bewitching with the reflection of the frescoed arcades shimmering in the water. History has bequeathed a number of great artists to the area, including Giorgione and Canova. As for its geographical position, Treviso is located within easy reach of the Prealpi, the foothills of the Alps and the Venetian lagoon and shares the climate and many of the customs of its more famous neighbour.

The city itself deserves a prolonged visit. The social and political center of the city is **Piazza dei Signori** where there are a variety of palaces including **Palazzo dei Trecento**, **Palazzo Podestà** which is surmounted by the *Torre Civica* and the Romanesque **Loggia dei Cavalieri**. **Palazzo dei Signori** is a crenelated 17th century building which now houses the High Council of the city, formed half by nobles and half by simple working people.

Connected to Piazza dei Signori is a little square known as Piazzetta del Monte di Pietà where the *Cappella dei Rettori* can be found, a small rectangular chapel with frescoes and an impressive ceiling. From here one

enters Piazza San Vito with its two adjoining medieval **churches**, **San Vito** and **Santa Lucia**, the latter being the most interesting. We then reach Piazza del Grano, now a lively market. (Also worth a visit for those who love markets is the famous nearby Pescheria, a lively fish market which takes place every morning on a small island).

Other notable religious buildings in Treviso include the **Duomo**, whose façade and interior is neoclassical while the foundations and crypt date back to the 11th century. The cathedral has a three-aisled interior and **Titian**'s splendid *Annunciation* hangs over the altar; there are also works by Girolamo da Treviso and Pietro Lombardo. Then there's the Romanesque-Gothic **church of San Francesco** which is famous for the illustrious tombs it contains; the **church of Santa Maria Maggiore**, known locally as "Madonna grande" and the **church of Santa Caterina**, destined to become a museum, which contains a cycle of frescoes by **Tommaso da Modena** depicting the *scenes from the life of Saint Ursula*.

The civil buildings of Treviso include a number of palaces whose façades are frescoed which are discussed in the inset on the facing page.

There are also examples of the Venetian style house owned by merchants which doubled up as a warehouse such as the Ca' dei Carraresi, once the residence of the noble family of that name.

Below: the Baptistery *and* Duomo *of Treviso.*
Below, left: an aerial view of the centro storico of the city and the Ponte San Francesco.

An exceptional museum

The **Pinacoteca of Treviso**, the city's art gallery, contains an abundance of great works of art. The gallery consists of thirty rooms where works of art are exhibited in chronological order, beginning with the 14th century work of Tommaso da Modena and climaxing in the stupendous achievements of the great Venetian painters. The gallery contains masterpieces by Giovanni Bellini, Cima da Conegliano, Lorenzo Lotto, Titian and Jacopo Bassano among others. Alongside a worthy collection of work from the 1600s, there's an abundance of masterpieces from the 1700s by Veneto artists such as Longhi, Rosalba Carriera and Giandomenico Tiepolo. The 1800 and 1900s are represented with works by Boldoni and many sculptures by Arturo Martini. The Pinacoteca also contains a curious but fascinating collection of publicity posters known as the "raccolta salce" which is the most extensive collection of its kind in Italy.

The masterpieces of the Pinacoteca

Above, clockwise:
unknown, Crucifix *(this work can be found in the* Museo Diocesano*);*
Giovanni Bellini, Madonna with Child;
Lorenzo Lotto, Portrait of a Domenic Monk.

The painted façades

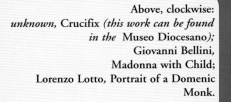

A characteristic of the palaces in Treviso is their frescoed façades. This form of decoration originated as a cheaper form of ornamentation than the decorative sculpture favored by the nobility. Artists were thus called upon to paint frescoes on the façades of homes. Treviso, in fact, has been defined urbs picta, or "the painted city". Splendid examples of this phenomenon can be admired in Via Sant'Agostino, Piazza Madonna Grande, Via Tolpada, Via Roma, Via Canova and Via Roggia.

Great food and wines of the "Marca felice"

Trevisan cuisine

The cuisine here is renowned and the red-leaved chicory and asparagus enjoy a far reaching fame. There are some excellent DOC cheeses. The wines are among the most well-known in Italy

The pride and joy of Trevisan cuisine is the red-leaved chicory. The *radicchio rosso* with its burgundy colored leaves is native to Treviso while the *radicchio variegato* with its large variegated leaves grows in the soil around Castelfranco Veneto. The former is on the bitter side while the latter tends to have a rather sweet taste. Annual fairs are dedicated to the chicory and master chefs have created entire menus around this unusual vegetable.

Also famous in Veneto is the *white asparagus* which in the Treviso region has a particularly delicate flavor and, together with the *green asparagus*, is marketed and exported here. Veneto is Italy's third largest regional producer of milk, sixty per cent of which is used in the production of the local cheeses. In the mountainous region a cheese called *Montasio DOC* is made which can either be eaten fresh or after it's been left to mature for a year or so. The hilly regions outside Treviso is where the cheese known as *Asiago DOC* is produced. Other highly recommended cheeses of the region include *Taleggio*, *Grana Padano* and *Provolone Val Padana*. On the plains a soft, fresh cheese "invented" by the villagers known as *Casatella* is produced.

A wine tasting tour

A series of wine tasting tours have been organized in the region known as "strade dei vini" which enable one to understand better the whole process of wine production in the area. For example, there's the *strada dei vini del Piave*, a circuitous tour of a flat area brimming with vineyards which produce both excellent red and white wines beginning and ending in Conegliano.

A recent addition is the *strada dei vini del Montello* and the *Asolani hills* which follows a route along the picturesque hilly strip of the Treviso region, passes through Montello, Caerano San Marco, Maser and winds up in Asolo. The wines proposed on this tour

include Merlot, Cabernet, Pinot Grigio and Bianco and Chardonnay.

A third tour for connoisseurs of wine is the *strada del Prosecco* which is forty even kilometers long and stretches from the hills of Conegliano to those of Valdobbiadene. Prosecco is discussed at greater length in the inset on the following page. Along this route there are also the cellars of authorized wines which bear the seal of approval shown in the photo.

An area where drink is an art

The Treviso area offers many excellent approved wines which bear the Doc certification. Let's single out a few from the long list. Among the high quality red wines of the Piave region there's Cabernet, Merlot, Pinot Nero, Raboso del Piave and Cabernet Sauvignon del Piave.

The best white wines include the delicate Verduzzo, Pinot Bianco, Pinot Grigio and the excellent Chardonnay del Piave. In the Montello and Asolani hills region the wines which deserve a special mention include Merlot, Cabernet, Pinot Bianco, Pinot Grigio and Chardonnay.

As for the Conegliano hills region, the Bianco Doc and Rosso Doc are both splendid wines as is the case with Torchiato di Fregona and Refrontolo Passito, the latter of especial interest because it is produced in very limited quantities.

Many organs, great music

A great school of organists (founded in the 18th century) have bequeathed to the city of Treviso and its provinces a number of splendid, still functioning organs. In the city itself one can admire and listen to these organs in various churches – the Cathedral, the churches of San Niccolò, San Gaetano, Sant'Agostino, San Leonardo and San Gregorio (photo below). Treviso is also part of the European Committee of cities with historic organs.

Conegliano, the Veneto capital of wine, nestling among splendid hills preserves masterpieces by Pordenone and Cima

Clockwise: Tower of the castle; Scuola dei Battuti *and the* campanile *of the* Duomo; *painting by* Cima da Conegliano *in the* Duomo.

Conegliano is a lively little town which has earned itself the accolade of Veneto's wine capital. Its two principle attractions are the old **Castle** which commands a splendid view over the surrounding countryside and the **Duomo** which contains some notable works of art. The 14th century **cathedral** has a large frescoed portico with nine arches while the naked simplicity of its interior contains masterpieces including paintings by **Palma il Giovane** and a wonderful *Madonna with Child and saints* by **Cima da Conegliano** (1493).

The castle dates back to the 10th century and is graced by two towers, *Torre Mozza* and *Torre della Campana* which is the home of the **Museo Civico** which contains paintings and frescoes by Palma il Giovane, Parmigianino and Pordenone.

Also worth a visit in Conegliano is the 15th century **house** where **Cima da Conegliano** was born and which now serves as a museum to the artist. Finally, there's the splendid frescoed **Scuola della Confraternita di S. Maria dei Battuti** which can be found near the Cathedral.

Where Prosecco rules

Valdebbiadene - not far from Vittorio Veneto – is the capital of two celebrated wines, Prosecco *and* Cartizze. *Here, every year, in the* Villa dei Cedri, *a national fair celebrating spumante, sparkling white wine, is held. The strada del Prosecco which is mentioned on the preceding page, passes through here. Nobody should leave the region without sampling at least a few of the varieties of Prosecco available: the* Prosecco tranquillo *for example which makes an ideal aperitif and should be served chilled; or the* Prosecco spumante, *a sparkling white wine. There's also the* Prosecco frizzante dolce, *a sweet sparkling white wine which makes an ideal companion to puddings. In the region of Cartizze, another very popular wine is produced – the* Prosecco superiore di Cartizze, *a pale-yellow colored fruity wine. Today Prosecco is the second most popular sparkling white wine in Italy, protected by a consortium and carrying a seal of certification on the bottle.*

A shoe market and a shoe museum

Within easy reach of Castelfranco is the lively town of Montebelluna which has earned itself the accolade of the world center for mountaineering boots. The town even possesses a museum dedicated to this article of footwear in the **Villa Binetti-Zuccareda**. Another interesting museum, the **Museo Civico Bellona**, housed in the splendid setting of the **Villa Biagi**, documents the palaeo-Venetic origins of the area. The nearby Colle del Montello warrants an excursion. For centuries its forests supplied the Venetian Republic with the wood for its ships. Today it is known for its many small restaurants where one can eat good traditional Veneto fare.

Above, left: *a section of the city wall*; right: *Giorgione's famous altarpiece.*

Castelfranco Veneto, elegant and intriguing with its red walls, luminous piazzas and the splendid painting by Giorgione

At the foot of the Asolane hills, Castelfranco is an old fortified town which offers a clean-cut tranquil atmosphere and various splendid works of art. Originally a Roman settlement, it became a town at the end of the 12th century and today still retains traces of its origins in the city walls and the castle. The **Cathedral**, on the other hand, is neoclassical and, besides works by Jacopo Bassano and Palma il Giovane, contains the magnificent altarpiece by **Giorgione** depicting the *Throned Madonna with Child and SS Liberale and Francis* (1504). A soft painted landscape surrounds the Virgin whose face wears a sad expression and whose eyes are lowered. Castelfranco preserves other memories of Giorgione – near the cathedral, there's the house

where he was believed to have lived (the life of Giorgione though remains clouded in mystery) and in Piazza Giorgione, also known as Piazza del Mercato, stands a monument to the great artist. In the same piazza one can also admire the **Loggia del Pavelon**. Other points of interest in the town are the **Teatro Accademico**, an elegantly harmonious 18th century building designed by **F.M. Preti** and the numerous historical palaces like **Palazzo Spinelli-Guidozzi**, **Casa Bovolini Soranzo** and **Palazzo Riccati Azzoni Avogadro**. In the environs of Castelfranco, at Treville, can be found the elegant Renaissance **Villa Corner Chiminelli**. In the small cemetery of San Vito of Altivole the architect Carlo Scarpa built a tomb to the Brion family.

Pinsa, zaleti, fregolotta and of course the chicory
Known as the "rose of Castelfranco", the legendary chicory

Castelfranco is well known for its gourmet restaurants and among the local specialities they serve up are a variety of rice dishes with, among other things, asparagus, mushrooms *and "lugànega", the local sausage. Other popular dishes include pasta with white "faggioli" beans, chicken "alla cacciatora",* tripe soup, polenta *and* baccalà. *But the pride and joy of the town's tables is the* chicory, *famous throughout the world. It becomes ripe during the winter, has a delicate taste and requires long and careful tending. Famous desserts of Castelfranco include* Pinsa, Zaleti *and* Fregolotta.

The Gipsoteca *in Possagno, a fascinating museum designed by the architect* Carlo Scarpa. Below: Villa Emo Capodilista*, in Fanzolo, another of* Palladio's *masterpieces.*

Palladio and Veronese at Villa Barbaro in Maser

Villa Barbaro in Maser is considered **Palladio**'s masterpiece and is also graced with splendid frescoes by Veronese (characterized by extraordinary visual effects, especially those in the *Sala dell'Olimpo*) and sculptures by Alessandro Vittoria. The harmony created by the villa's architecture and the surrounding countryside is exemplary and creates a stunning visual feast. The room known as the "Salone delle feste" is particularly impressive, looking out as it does on a bewitching rural panorama.

Asolo

Beautiful landscapes, elegant frescoed houses and a rich artistic heritage characterize the charming town of Asolo. The town's main square, Piazza Maggiore, has an old Roman fountain, the 15th century **Loggia del Capitano** and the picturesque **Villa Pisani**. The town was famous during the Renaissance for being the home of Caterina Cornaro, the Queen of Cyprus who lived in the castle with her court. Overlooking the town is the **Rocca**, a polygonal fortress which has recently been restored and is one of the most impressive buildings in the entire region. The **Cathedral** is also worth a visit with works by Lotto and Jacopo Bassano.

Outside Asolo, at Maser, is the stupendous **Villa Barbaro**, widely considered one of **Andrea Palladio**'s masterpieces which also contains frescoes by Paolo Veronese. Palladio also designed the nearby **Tempietto**. Also worth visiting is the fascinating **Museo delle carrozze antiche**, a museum dedicated to old carriages.

Possagno

Eight kilometers from Asolo is Possagno, native town of the great 18th century sculptor Antonio Canova and famous for its **Tempio di Canova** designed with great originality by the sculptor on the model of the Greco-Roman pantheon.

The building dominates the town and contains work by Canova himself including the *Pietà* as well as the artist's tomb.

Other worthwhile points of interest offered by the town include, in the town center, the **Casa di Canova**, the artist's home and, next door, the **Gipsoteca** which contains casts of many of the sculptor's great works and is a fine museum designed by Carlo Scarpa.

The most beautiful villas of the province

In the area known as the "Marca Trevigiana" there's a profusion of Veneto villas numbering more than seven hundred. Three of these were designed by Palladio: *the* Villa Barbaro *at Maser, the* Villa Emo Capodilista *at Fanzolo di Vedelago and* Villa Zeno *at Donegal di Cessalto. Other surviving examples of the stunningly beauty and harmony with the surrounding landscape achieved by many of these villas include* Villa Giustinian *in Portobuffolè,* Villa Toderini *in Codognè,* Villa Franchetti *in Preganziol and* Villa Papadopoli *in San Paolo di Piave. However, it would be impossible to list all of the villas in the region which merit a visit and enhance the exceptional beauty of the countryside in which they've been set. Some great architects have had a hand in designing many of the villas in the Treviso area, including Baldassarre Longhena, Francesco Maria Preti, Girolamo Frigimelica and Giorgio Massari.*

INDEX

VERONA (142)

BELLUNO (170)

DOLOMITES (180)

TREVISO (184)